MONTANA GREATS

MONTANA GREATS

From A (Absarokee) to Z (Zurich),
the greatest athletes from 264 Montana communities

JEFF WELSCH

EXECUTIVE SPORTS EDITOR, 406MTSPORTS.COM
AND LEE MONTANA NEWSPAPERS

RIVERBEND
PUBLISHING

AUTHOR'S NOTE:

While we have made every effort at factual and contextual accuracy in *Montana Greats*, it's possible some information was initially incorrect or has changed through the years, or we simply erred. To correct mistakes, provide updates, or nominate a Great for future editions (especially from communities that are not included here), please contact author Jeff Welsch at jeff.welsch@406mtsports.com.

Montana Greats: From A (Absarokee) to Z (Zurich)

Published by Riverbend Publishing, Helena, Montana

ISBN: 978-1-60639-129-7

Printed in the USA

1 2 3 4 5 6 7 8 MG 26 25 24 23 22 21

Cover and text design by Sarah Cauble, sarahcauble.com

Riverbend Publishing
P.O. Box 5833
Helena, MT 59604
1-406-449-0200
riverbendpublishing.com

Contents

Preface

A CHANCE ENCOUNTER IN TERRY

After pedaling bicycles some 15 dusty miles under an unforgiving sun—half of it on teeth-chattering gravel—my wife, Sherry, and I had a singular mission on a toasty eastern Montana afternoon in the summer of 2019.

A cold beverage.

That trail of cheers led us to the 4 Corners Convenience Store in Terry, a busy little hub in an otherwise sedate ag community squeezed between Interstate 94 and the burly Yellowstone River, a fossil's toss from the ghostly humps and hoodoos of the Terry Badlands.

Sitting in a shaded area out front, selling shaved ice to parched passersby, were the store's owner, Leann Lantis, and her daughter Laiten, one of the town's more gifted athletes.

After introductions, conversation ensued, one sports topic led to another, and upon discovering that Leann had lived, played and coached in Terry for 46 years, I thought her a perfect foil for a question I'd been asking from border to border for months.

Who is the greatest athlete born, raised or otherwise associated with your town?

Since December 2018, I'd combed the Internet, newspaper archives, books and museums as well as interviewed friends, colleagues, acquaintances and longtime Treasure State sports aficionados to determine the same answer for (nearly) every Montana community from A (Absarokee) to Z (Zurich).

In describing the project, I noted I already had a credible

prospect for Terry. But as I'd repeatedly discovered, overturning one rock often led to another and then to another and then another.

Leann hemmed and hawed. Her mind peeled back the years.

Finally, a name: Scott Eaton, a four-sport athlete in the late 1980s who earned a football scholarship to Montana State University.

I nodded. In our tiniest communities, too many of which have long since bolted their high school's doors or co-opted with neighboring schools due to population drain, that was often a winner's resume.

Having already written short bios for well over 200 Montana Greats (now 263), I couldn't immediately recall my Terry pick. I tapped my phone for my list and saw that I had another former Terriers football star, Ryan Herman, whose name dots the Montana High School Association record books.

Leann nodded as I listed Herman's exploits.

"Can't go wrong there either," we simultaneously agreed.

A few more minutes of chatter passed before Leann excitedly interrupted the nostalgia.

"Well, here comes the greatest of all time right now!" she exclaimed.

I looked toward the gas pumps to see an athletic 30-something woman striding our way. A decade after the end of her collegiate playing days, Lacey Haughian still looked as if she could dominate the paint on a basketball court, toss a javelin a country mile and wrestle a hapless steer to the dirt.

As Haughian approached, Leann rattled off her many accomplishments in basketball and track, highlighted by her first-team All-America hoops honors at Black Hills State University in South Dakota and subsequent career in Sweden, Finland and Germany.

"Our only professional athlete," Leann concluded, bringing down the proverbial gavel on Terry's "Great."

In short order we learned Haughian was running her family cattle ranch and working summers as a Bureau of Land Management ranger. She still played basketball and tapped up a Twitter video on her phone of a game-winning shot she made to secure a championship in Germany.

I marveled at my small-world good fortune.

I also winced.

So, I suddenly surmised, the only surefire way to conduct this project was to stop for a beverage in every community hub, chat up the local social nexus and hope the greatest of all time steps out of a pickup truck.

Yeah.

Thus, despite nearly two years of relentless sleuthing, the lengthy list of Greats in this book certainly could be imperfect—though when it first appeared at 406mtsports.com and in Lee Montana newspapers in November 2019 I was gratified to learn I had "whiffed badly" on only one community. The remaining disputes were the type of barstool debates I'd sought.

Though every Montana community that has had a high school as well as a population listed on the official state map is represented, unearthed treasures from tiny outposts surely remain. Some of our current choices likely could shift from towns where they starred in high school to the nearby map dots where they actually lived.

Indeed, it was what to do with two-time world bull-riding champion Jess Lockwood that advanced this project beyond the roughly 150 communities with high schools. Lockwood attended high school in Broadus, but by any reckoning he is a Volborg cowboy.

As such, and with additions and revisions surely in the Greats' future, we welcome hearing from readers with suggestions for filling in even more blanks.

After all, as we discovered on a parched July afternoon in eastern Montana, when we went looking for a cold beverage and stumbled upon Terry's "Great," local institutional knowledge is second only to being there.

Jeff Welsch

Introduction

A 21-month labor of enlightenment began on a whim in late 2018, with an impromptu urge to veer off a busy highway and see what remained of a once-bustling mining town that for most folks is little more than a sign—"RADERSBURG 9"—beckoning 70-mph travelers on U.S. Highway 287 between Townsend and Three Forks.

Turns out there isn't much at the end of those nine miles of lonely pavement: A few well-manicured homes under canopies of mature trees, a 1917 church at a slight elbow in the road midtown, a restored century-old ranger station across from a schoolhouse receiving similar TLC, creaky wood remnants of a bygone Masonic Lodge and two-story hotel, and the beginning of a gravel road that rises into juniper and scrub hills before vanishing into the mysterious. On the eastern edge of town, a sign in Boot Hill-style lettering points toward the Radersburg Cemetery and memories of a bygone era.

You can easily walk from one end of town to the other and not see any of the 75 souls who call gold miner Rueben Rader's 1866 creation along Crow Creek home.

"If you blink twice, you'll miss it," says Dan Williams, vice president of Radersburg Historical Preservation Inc.

Poke around just a bit, though, and you'll make some astonishing discoveries.

For instance, Myrna Loy, the "Queen of Hollywood" for appearing in more than 150 films over six decades beginning in the 1920s, was raised in Radersburg as Myrna Williams.

President Ulysses S. Grant once arrived in a stagecoach and stayed overnight in one of the three hotels, back when the population was more than 2,000 and Radersburg was Montana's second-largest mining town. A local lawyer named George Cowan was among tourists captured by fleeing Nez Perce Indians in Yellowstone National Park in 1877, six weeks before Chief Joseph poignantly conceded he would "fight no more forever."

And then there's Cecil Elba "Larry" Duff.

A strapping 6-foot-1 lad, Duff was a right-handed pitcher and left-handed hitter who spent 16 days with the Chicago White Sox in September 1922, three years after the infamous Black Sox Scandal. His record was 1-1 and he struck out seven in a career barely longer than Moonlight Graham's of *Field of Dreams* fame.

Duff was born in Radersburg on Nov. 20, 1896, at the end of the gold and silver boom. By then, the town had lost the Jefferson County seat to Boulder, after the Northern Pacific Railroad opted to hug the Missouri River nine miles—might as well have been 900—to the east.

That such an accomplished athlete had come from Radersburg, of all places, set me to wondering.

What other treasures must there be from towns across Montana, large and small, thriving or shrinking? Who are the Treasure State's other Larry Duffs?

The results are found on these pages: Montana's Greats from (nearly) every town—264 and counting—from A (Absarokee) to Z (Zurich).

The initial aim was to find the Great from every community with a high school. But along the way, we discovered standouts from towns that are little more than a single dusty dot on a dirt road—or, in one case, Two Dot.

We think you'll marvel at Montana's mother lode of athletes and their stories.

Did you know, for instance, that a touted baseball player who would as a scout "discover" future Chicago Cubs Hall of Famer Ernie Banks was the "Pride of Plevna"?

Did you know that a 1956 Olympic boxer once featured in a *Sports Illustrated* story grew up in Opportunity? Or that the "Montana cowboy" who Muhammad Ali credited with hitting him the hardest, knocking him to the canvas, was reared in the Bull Mountains near Musselshell?

Raise your hand if you are aware the world's fastest human in the early 1960s—before "Bullet" Bob Hayes of Dallas Cowboys fame stole the mantle, rendering him merely "the world's fastest white man"—was Livingston born and raised.

Pat yourself on the back if your reservoir of Montana sporting knowledge includes the first and last purveyor of college football's innovative "hidden-ball trick" of 1903: A speedy Carlisle (Pa.) Indian School lineman of Sioux descent who called Wyola home.

And how about the National Basketball Association's first legally deaf player, a dual citizen of Mexico and the U.S. whose early years were spent in a fundamentalist polygamist Mormon community in the Bitterroot Valley?

Along this road to discovery, our digging reopened our eyes to communities that once boasted Class C basketball powerhouses but have since shuttered their school's doors: Antelope, Bearcreek, Flaxville, Hogeland, Outlook and Peerless, to name a few.

Former high school stars in traditional sports dominate our selections, but we also have rodeo cowboys and cowgirls, Olympians in events from rowing to rifle to skiing, a few mushers and even a Herculean body builder once described by a fellow Mr. America as "the best-looking, best-built man God has ever created."

We even considered a horse: "Spokane," the only Montana-born thoroughbred to win the Kentucky Derby (1889). Spokane's journey to fame began in a round barn two miles north of Twin Bridges.

Many Montana legends aren't included simply because our largest cities have so many choices. Fortunately, in many cases athletes routinely associated with, say, Billings, Great Falls or Missoula actually lived in smaller communities on the fringes—think Carter, Lockwood, Huntley, Vida, St. Xavier and Bonner, among others.

To that end, if you come across a town and think we've missed the mark—say, Chinook—be sure to stay with us to the literal end.

In ultimately determining a single "Great," many factors were considered: Number of sports played, levels reached, impact on the state, national or world stage, and even the "it" factor.

Simply being born in Montana was neither a qualification nor a requirement.

Legendary NBA player and coach Phil Jackson, born in Deer Lodge, was trumped by an athlete whose name has more Montana staying power. Ditto for Wolf Point's John Lowenstein—the only Montana native to appear in at least 1,000 Major League Baseball games—who was born on the Hi-Line but moved away as a toddler.

Simply passing through Montana for the proverbial cup of coffee didn't rank, either.

For example, John Elway, the Hall of Fame quarterback, spent a portion of his childhood in Missoula but isn't thought of as a Montanan. Conversely, though Green Bay Packers

Hall of Famer Jerry Kramer (spoiler alert!) only had his first six years in Montana, five in Jordan, his impact in Garfield County is lasting; a street honors his family and he named one of his sons after the town.

You'll surely marvel at much of the Montana athletic gold we've unearthed. You'll just as surely argue some of the selections.

That's partly the point.

Montana Greats is designed to be a conversation starter and a way to showcase the Treasure State's treasure trove of athletes, from thriving urban areas such as Billings, Missoula and Bozeman to nearly forgotten outposts like Radersburg.

Enjoy—and let the debates begin!

Absarokee

LAURA DANIEL (ARTHUN)

TRACK AND FIELD

A pole vaulter, Daniel won three consecutive state championships from 1995-97 and still has the fourth and seventh best marks in Montana history (10-3 and 10-9). She also was an exceptional hurdler and as a junior sang the national anthem to start the Class C state meet not long before tying her state pole vault mark. As Laura Daniel-Arthun at Oral Roberts University in Oklahoma, she went on to become the Mid-Continent Conference indoor pole vault champion in 1997-98 and again in 2000-01, and also was the 1998 outdoor champion. She was the league's Newcomer of the Year for the 1997-98 indoor season and competed for four years. Today, Daniel-Arthun coaches at Manhattan Christian.

Alberton

K.C. McGOWAN

BASKETBALL

An all-round athlete, McGowan was a high school All-American in both basketball and track, first in his hometown of Alberton and then at Missoula Big Sky, where he transferred for a better shot at fulfilling his dream of playing college hoops. He went on to play for Montana and early in his career also competed in track as a high jumper, earning the basketball program's Most Inspirational Player Award in 1988 and '89. McGowan finished his high school career with 1,943 points, a 21.6 average over four seasons. At Montana, he finished his career among the school's top 25 scorers. McGowan lives in the Seattle area, where he has worked in the financial services industry and coaches youth basketball.

Alder

PETE ANDERSON

FOOTBALL

An all-stater in basketball, football and track, Anderson was a key cog in Twin Bridges' 2009 state Class C hoops title. He scored 12 points in the Falcons' 63-61 win over Box Elder for the crown. In football he was an all-conference fullback/tailback and linebacker, and in track he was a champion shot putter. Anderson took football to the next level, starting as a linebacker and running back for Rocky Mountain College, where he routinely found the end zone. Anderson worked in the agriculture industry after graduating and now is a financial advisor in Great Falls.

Alzada

LARRY SANDVICK

RODEO

A native of North Dakota's Little Missouri River Badlands country just across the border, Sandvick made his home outside of Alzada when he was one of the top bareback riders in the country in the late 1990s and early 2000s. He finished fourth in the National Finals Rodeo in his 1992 debut and qualified for 12 NFRs overall. Sandvick also competed for the U.S. against Canada in the 2002 Salt Lake City Olympics, and was PRCA Mountain States Circuit all-around cowboy in 1995 and 1998. Sandvick, who now lives near Kaycee, Wyoming, and owns a leather business, was inducted into North Dakota's Cowboy Hall of Fame in 2018.

Amsterdam

JOHN WEIDENAAR

FOOTBALL

A member of a large farm family west of Belgrade, Weidenaar was an all-state offensive and defensive lineman as well as punter for a Manhattan-Manhattan Christian co-op. He also excelled in track and field, where he was solid in the discus and shot put while also running on the Tigers' relay team, and he played basketball for both Manhattan and Manhattan Christian. Weidenaar went on to play left tackle at Montana State, where he started 49 consecutive games—a record that stood until Mitch Brott broke it in 2019. Weidenaar signed as an undrafted free agent with the Cincinnati Bengals in 2016 and played in four preseasons games before getting cut. A neck fracture suffered in a car accident ended his football career. He lives in Bozeman, where he is a sales rep for John Deere.

Anaconda

WAYNE ESTES

BASKETBALL

Perhaps no Montana sports story is more tragic than Estes, a beloved all-round athlete who died in a bizarre electrocution on a street in Logan, Utah, within hours of setting Utah State's season scoring record in 1965. A night earlier, the Aggies' big man had proposed to his longtime girlfriend in Provo, Utah. The nation's No. 2 collegiate scorer that season behind Miami's Rick Barry, Estes had been told by the Los Angeles Lakers that they planned to make him their No. 1 draft choice. The basketball practice facility at Utah State is named for him and he was a member of the Aggies' inaugural Hall of Fame class in 1993. At Anaconda, Estes was an all-state athlete in football, basketball and track—winning the state discus and shot put championships. He still holds the Copperheads' shot put record. Estes was out with friends and was walking on a sidewalk past the scene of a car accident on that tragic night when a low-hanging power line creased his forehead. He is buried in a cemetery outside of Anaconda.

Antelope

HARVEY LEE

BASKETBALL

Antelope once had a proud sports tradition and no one represented it better than Lee, who averaged 22.7 points per game and was Class C all-state in 1975. The forward scored 33 points in the opening game of the state tournament against Hysham in '75. After leading the Pronghorns to the title game, Lee was state champion in the high hurdles and third in the low hurdles in the spring. A native of Kalispell, Lee also was an outstanding baseball player. He eventually earned a teaching degree from Eastern Montana College. Lee died in 2018.

Photo: Harvey Lee, No. 40, back row, fourth from left.

Arlee

RACHAEL MYLLYMAKI

RODEO

A national high school all-around champion in 1994-95, Myllymaki earned national acclaim—including a piece in *People* magazine—when she qualified for the Wrangler National Finals Rodeo as an 11-year-old barrel racer in 1988. As the second-youngest competitor ever at the NFR, she finished ninth in the world standings. Myllymaki would qualify for the NFR six more times, win two Dodge National Circuit Finals titles, and set a Northern Rodeo Association record for single-season earnings. She also competed collegiately at Montana and Montana Western, where she won national all-around and barrel-racing crowns. Myllymaki was a nine-time year-end Montana Pro Rodeo Circuit Finals champion. A 1995 Arlee High graduate, she eventually moved to Simi Valley, California.

Ashland

GEORGE YELLOW EYES

BASKETBALL

Some say Yellow Eyes was the greatest outside shooter in state history, and wonder what kind of numbers he'd have put up if the 3-point line existed in Montana in the late 1950s. He grew up on the Northern Cheyenne Reservation but played high school ball for the State Industrial School in Miles City, scoring 46 points in one game and 103 in three games in the 1959 Class C tournament. In all, Yellow Eyes scored 1,450 points for the State Industrial School for a 19.3 average over four years, scoring 711 points in 1958-59 alone. A two-time all-state selection in high school, Yellow Eyes averaged 24 points per game his first year at Miles Community but was injured fighting fires the following summer and never regained his basketball skills. He was inducted into the Montana Indian Athletic Hall of Fame in 2009. Yellow Eyes moved for a time to the San Carlos Apache reservation in Arizona. He died in 1990 at age 50 shortly after a construction accident.

Augusta

MICHEALA HOWE-COBB

BASKETBALL

Take a look at the state record books for blocked shots, and one name stands out—15 times. That's the number of slots Howe-Cobb holds for blocks in a single game, from her record of 16 set in 2007-08—and matched the next season—down to the six times she recorded 11. Not surprisingly, Howe-Cobb holds the state's career blocked-shots record (455) and three of the top five single-season marks (207, 145 and 103). The 6-1 post averaged a triple-double as a sophomore and still holds the state record for rebounds in a game with 37. She went on to sign with MSU-Northern, where she was a scholar-athlete. Now Michaela Whitmore, she graduated from the University of Washington School of Medicine and is a physician's assistant in Havre.

Avon

MAC BIGNELL

FOOTBALL

Bignell is a big name in a big state, and none are any bigger than Mac, who was a dominant athlete at small-school powerhouse Drummond and then was a standout linebacker after walking on at Montana State. He was a star quarterback and basketball player for the Trojans, once scoring seven touchdowns against Arlee and 41 points in a hoops game against Victor. A captain for the Bobcats, he led the team in tackles for three years running. Bignell earned all-Big Sky honors as a junior and preseason All-America accolades as a senior. In 2018, he received a minicamp invitation from the Philadelphia Eagles of the NFL.

Bainville

CHANCE HYATT

CROSS COUNTRY

Accomplished in cross country in the fall and distance running in the spring, Hyatt etched Bainville's name in the MHSA record books by winning back-to-back Class C cross country titles with a Culbertson-Bainville co-op in 2012 and 2013. As a senior, he won by 35 seconds. In the spring, he was highly competitive in the 800, 1,600 and 3,200 meters—winning all three at the Eastern C meet in 2014. No slouch on the basketball court, Hyatt occasionally put up a 20-point night. He went on to run at Carroll College, where he was two-time Frontier Conference cross country champion and earned All-American honors for the third consecutive fall with his 21st-place finish at the national NAIA meet in November 2018.

Baker

SHANN SCHILLINGER

FOOTBALL

A three-sport standout with the Spartans, Schillinger—a sprinter and hurdler in track—would go on to star as a free safety at Montana, including playing in two national championship games as a defensive back. As a high school quarterback, he compiled more than 1,700 yards and 29 touchdowns as a senior either throwing or running the ball. By the time he'd used up his eligibility, Schillinger ranked 20th all-time in tackles for the Griz. In 2010, he was drafted by the Atlanta Falcons and would play four years with two NFL teams. Reportedly and ironically named for former MSU basketball player Shann Ferch, Schillinger later coached briefly at Nebraska before moving on to his current position as an assistant at his alma mater.

Ballantine

JEN WALTER

TRACK AND FIELD

One of the most decorated athletes in Huntley Project history, Walter was a 16-time Class B champion as a sprinter, hurdler and in relays. She was a four-time winner in the 100 dash and 330 hurdles and a three-time winner in the 200 and 400, earning 23 state medals overall, as HP won state titles in 2004, 2006 and 2007. Walter also played for three state volleyball title teams and was Class B MVP as a senior. At Montana, the Lodge Grass native was a four-time all-conference performer in track as a hurdler and sprinter from 2007-11. Walter currently lives in Billings.

Bearcreek

MIKE AND JOHN BAROVICH

BASKETBALL

Photo: Mike Barovich

Back when the Smith Mine was humming, Bearcreek was a state power and the Barovich brothers from Serbia were the stars. John was an all-state center in 1932, went on to play at Montana State College and eventually coached in Columbus and Miles City. Mike turned down out-of-state offers to play at Billings Polytechnical Institute, now Rocky Mountain College. Mike lettered in basketball, football, baseball and track, and led the Crusaders (now Battlin' Bears) to a 21-1 record in 1938-39. He won three league titles at BPI and is credited by some with inventing the hook shot—he used it repeatedly, from long range—made famous later by Kareem Abdul-Jabbar. As for John, after leaving coaching, he became a private pilot and was so infamous for accidents the FAA printed a book called *This Is Your Life John Barovich*. He later took up golf, which he played competitively almost until his death at age 92 in 2006. Mike, who also became a standout senior golfer, died in 2010. The brothers, who lived in Billings, were preceded in death by their father, Simo, in the 1943 Smith Mine Disaster.

Belfry

WALT LINDERMAN

RODEO

A member of one of the state's two most famous rodeo families—the Greenoughs being the other—Linderman became a professional cowboy immediately after graduating from Belfry High School. In the 1960s and '70s, he was a consistent competitor in steer wrestling at the National Finals Rodeo, qualifying nine times. Linderman won the NFR steer wrestling title in 1967 and was second in the world standings three times. He was champion at most of the major rodeos in North America, including the Calgary Stampede and Pendleton Round-Up. Linderman also competed in saddle bronc and bareback riding, and he owned a steer wrestling horse named Scottie that won three world titles, had six NFR average crowns and was enshrined into the Montana State Rodeo Hall of Fame in 2015. Linderman was inducted into the National Cowboy Hall of Fame in Oklahoma City in 2016. He died in 2005 at age 69.

Belgrade

SARAH FLOCK (FOWLER)

BASKETBALL

Some would argue that Flock is the greatest player in Montana State basketball history after she became the first ever at the school to earn first-team all-Big Sky Conference honors three times. She also is the only three-time MVP in Bobcat history, winning from 1990-92. Flock still ranks fourth or better in 10 statistical categories, including scoring average. A Kodak All-America honorable mention selection in 1992, she was inducted into the MSU Hall of Fame in 2003 and most recently coached Belgrade High girls basketball. As an athlete at Belgrade, she was an all-round standout, earning all-state honors in basketball and volleyball while also competing as a sprinter and hurdler in track.

Belt

TURK LORDS

WRESTLING

Lords lived with his grandparents so he could wrestle for Great Falls CMR, where he won two Class AA state championships before moving on to an illustrious career at MSU-Northern after transferring from Montana Western. He won four consecutive NAIA championships (1998-2001) and led the Lights to three national team crowns. In 2001, he was selected NAIA outstanding wrestler after completing his career with a 126-10 record—losing only to NCAA Division I opposition. Lords also was a Junior National Greco-Roman champion and freestyle runner-up in 1995, and had dreams of wrestling in the Olympics in Greco-Roman.

Bigfork

MAKENA MORLEY

CROSS COUNTRY

A four-time state cross country champion and two-time All-American with the Vikings, Morley's feet took her to another level in college. After winning the Big Sky Conference crown in her lone year at Montana, she transferred to Colorado, where she was a seven-time All-American and helped lead the Buffaloes to their third NCAA women's cross country title in 2018. In track, Morley was a three-time first-team All-American and three-time second-team All-American between the 3,000, 5000 and 10,000 meters indoors and outdoors; she owns the Buffaloes' school record in the 10,000, is third in the 3,000 and third in the indoor 5,000. Morley spent her first collegiate year at Montana, where she was Big Sky cross country champion in her third career race. At Bigfork, she was a state champ in the 3,200 (twice), 1,600 and 800 to earn All-America distinction three times.

Big Sandy

LARRY KANE

RODEO

Back in the 1960s and '70s, Kane was something of a legend on the rodeo circuit after earning Rodeo Cowboys Association Rookie of the Year in 1960. The saddle bronc rider—nicknamed "Mighty Little Giant"—qualified for the National Finals Rodeo for four consecutive years (1960-63), finishing as high as second in 1961. Kane also solidified his legend status by staying aboard the notorious Descent—the six-time bucking horse of the year—all four times he rode the famous horse. Kane later worked as a pickup man at the NFR. He was inducted into the Rodeo Cowboy Hall of Fame in 2010. Kane died in 2008 at age 70. A large granite memorial along U.S. 87 in Big Sandy acknowledges a hometown hero.

Big Sky

KEELY KELLEHER

SKIING

Despite numerous injuries, Kelleher—who grew up along the Gallatin River just north of Big Sky—was U.S. National Super G champion in 2010, beating a host of Olympians. She was an alternate for the Winter Olympics in Vancouver, B.C., that year. In 2007 she finished eighth at the U.S. Alpine Championships and in 2008 she made the U.S. national alpine team. Kelleher was on the U.S. ski team for eight years, competing in the downhill and Super G. She also starred in two Warren Miller films and in 2011 started Keely's Camp For Girls at Mount Bachelor in Oregon. The camp has since expanded to other ski communities, including Jackson, Wyoming, where she now lives.

Big Timber

TIM HAUCK

FOOTBALL

Famous for his bone-jarring hits, Hauck was the reason the No. 37 has reached mythical status at Montana. An all-stater as a quarterback and defensive back at Big Timber, he walked on with the Griz after a year at Oregon's Pacific University and became a two-time All-American free safety in the late 1980s. Nicknamed "Hitter," he spent 13 seasons as a defensive back in the NFL with seven teams. After his playing career was over, he coached at Montana and was an assistant on the Philadelphia Eagles' Super Bowl championship team in 2018. At Big Timber, Hauck set the state Class B record in the pole vault in 1985 with a leap of 14-4 and he was a high-scoring starter on the Herders' basketball team. He is enshrined in the Montana Football Hall of Fame.

Billings

DAVE McNALLY

BASEBALL

A crafty left-hander, McNally was part of what many consider to be the greatest starting pitching staff in Major League Baseball history with the Baltimore Orioles of the late 1960s and early '70s. He played 13 years in the Majors, was a 20-game winner four times, and remains the only pitcher ever to hit a grand slam in a World Series (1970). McNally won 184 games in 14 seasons. He also made history by helping to overturn baseball's reserve clause, ultimately resulting in the genesis of free agency. Playing American Legion ball in Billings, McNally led his team to a national runner-up finish. In its December 1999 list of the top 50 athletes from each state, *Sports Illustrated* declared McNally No. 1 in Montana. He died of cancer in 2002.

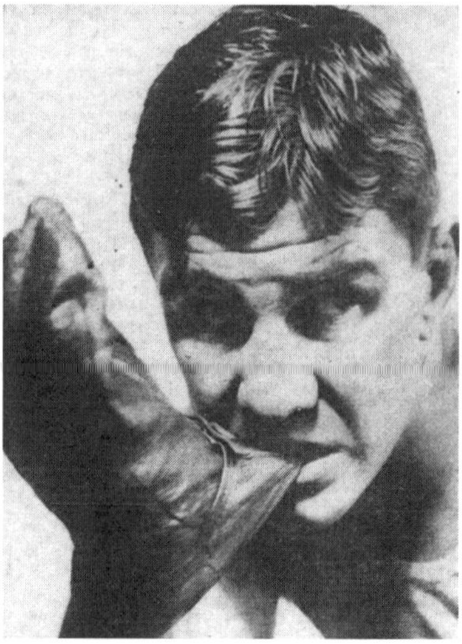

Bonner

RITCHIE FONTAINE

BOXING

The little onetime sawmill town at the confluence of the Blackfoot and Clark Fork rivers was known for its tough guys, none tougher than Fontaine. Nicknamed the "Bonner Buzzsaw," he was Montana featherweight champion and a successful professional boxer in the 1930s. Fontaine is remembered mostly for being the last fighter to beat future lightweight world champion Henry Armstrong, who ESPN ranks as the third greatest fighter of all time. Born in 1916 in Fairview, Fontaine was a featherweight who was 40-28-11 for his career, with 15 knockouts. He beat Armstrong on a TKO in Seattle in 1939. In 1941, his management was taken over by the comedy team of Abbott and Costello and he moved to Hollywood. Fontaine, who after World War II opened a super club east of Missoula called The Ring (later Club Chateau), died of a heart attack in a Los Angeles hotel in 1963 at age 47.

Boulder

CRISTIE BELL

BASKETBALL

Bell did it all for Jefferson High School, where she excelled in basketball and track. In the spring, she was a top-flight javelin thrower, shot putter and won gold in the hammer in all-comers meets. Bell continued to thrive in both sports at Rocky Mountain College, where she was a Frontier Conference and NAIA district champion in the shot put, qualifying for nationals and finishing ninth in 1986. She also was a standout basketball player for the Battlin' Bears. Bell, a co-captain in basketball and track, later served as Rocky's football trainer before becoming an Internet engineer and moving to Portland, Oregon. She was inducted into the Rocky Hall of Fame in 1999.

Box Elder

LEANN MONTES

BASKETBALL

Born on the Rocky Boy Reservation, Montes averaged 21 points, 10 rebounds and eight steals per game in leading Box Elder to its first Class C girls basketball crown in 1998. She was MVP in the state and an All-American on two lists. Montes continued her career at Montana, where she played from 1999-2003. In her final season, the former walk-on ranked third in the Big Sky in assist-to-turnover ratio and was ninth in assists. Montes, who went to law school at the University of New Mexico, became attorney general for the Chippewa-Cree tribe. She also coached at Stone Child College at Rocky Boy Agency. Montes was inducted into the Montana Indian Athletic Hall of Fame in 2014.

Bozeman

COREY WIDMER

FOOTBALL

Born in Virginia, Widmer was a standout defensive lineman at Bozeman High and went on to become a two-time second-team All-American at Montana State (1990-91). He was the Big Sky Conference's defensive MVP in 1990 when he had 25 tackles for losses and played in the Hula Bowl. His 66 career tackles for losses are a school record, and he ranks fourth in sacks. Widmer was then a seventh-round draft choice of the New York Giants of the NFL in 1992, spending eight years as a linebacker before retiring in 1999—a year after suffering a severe concussion. He was inducted in MSU's Hall of Fame in 2002 and has since become a critic of the NFL's approach toward concussion mitigation and CTE. Widmer now lives primarily in Las Vegas, Nevada.

Brady

DAN SIELER

FOOTBALL

Before Brady consolidated with Dutton, the Bulldogs were a 6-Man program and Sieler was one of its finest stars, having earned all-state honors on both sides of the ball and serving as the team's quarterback for four years (1995-98). In a game against Rocky Boy in 1996, Sieler threw a school-record 10 TD passes. He also was a solid basketball player for Brady, routinely scoring in double figures as starting point guard.

Bridger

BILL LINDERMAN

RODEO

Raised mostly in Red Lodge, Linderman was the face of Montana rodeo in the 1940s and '50s when he was the official Rodeo Cowboys Association All-Around Cowboy twice (1950, 1953) and unofficial winner once (1945). In 1950, he became the first cowboy to win three national titles in a single year and was also the first to win more than $500,000. In all, Linderman won six world championships, including two in saddle bronc riding and one each in bareback and steer wrestling. Always dreaming of a postseason event, Linderman saw his vision come to fruition in 1959 with the creation of the annual National Finals Rodeo; he qualified for the first NFR that year but withdrew to focus on making the event successful. He was inducted into the ProRodeo Hall of Fame in 1979, 14 years after dying in a plane crash in Salt Lake City. A statue of Linderman greets visitors at the Hall of Fame in Oklahoma City.

Broadus

RONNIE ROSSEN

BULL RIDING

A native of Nebraska, Rossen was known as one of the most fearless bull riders on the circuit and won world championships in 1961 and 1966. He appeared in eight National Finals Rodeo events from 1959-68, narrowly missing a third crown in 1965. En route to his '61 buckle, he became the first rider in six years to stay aboard the notorious Speck. Rossen went on to ride for 40 years, winning seven National Old Timers Rodeo crowns before dying in 1991 when he was caught under a bull during his dismount from a winning ride. He was inducted in the ProRodeo Hall of Fame in 2007.

Broadview

MONICA TRANEL

ROWING

Go figure—an Olympic rower from a tiny landlocked ag community in central Montana. But that's just what Tranel is, winning a gold medal with the U.S. eights crew at the 1995 world championships, taking three silvers, picking up one bronze, and finishing fourth at the 1996 Olympics in Atlanta. In all, she has won 10 national rowing titles. Born in Big Horn, Wyoming, Tranel also competed in the 2000 Olympics. She attended high school at Billings Central, where she starred in basketball and track. She started rowing in college at Gonzaga and earned a law degree from Rutgers; a lawyer, she has lived in Helena and now Missoula, where she has run for public office.

Brockton

KAYLA LAMBERT

BASKETBALL

An absolute scoring machine, Lambert finished her career with the Warriors as by far the leading career scorer in Montana history—boy or girl—with 3,453 points in 101 games (1998-2001), 900 better than any other girl. She averaged a whopping 34.2 points per game in high school and was Gatorade Player of the Year twice, scoring 65 points in a game two times and setting a state mark with 66 in 2000. Lambert, the first Native American girl to be invited to the Nike All-American Camp, once had a quadruple-double: 51 points, 15 rebounds, 10 steals, 10 assists. Recruited by Big Ten, ACC and Pac-10 schools, the Bozeman native chose Montana and sat out a season before becoming academically ineligible and enrolling at Sheridan (Wyoming) College. Lambert tried to reinvigorate her basketball career in 2007 at Lethbridge College in Alberta, Canada. In 2016, she was inducted into the Montana Indian Athletic Hall of Fame.

Brockway

OLE UELAND

TRACK AND FIELD

The patriarch of the famed Ueland family better known for the Butte area, Ole was an all-American in the 880-yard run from 1937 to 1939 at the University of Montana. He was captain of the track team that was coached by the legendary Harry Adams. Ole was nicknamed "Iron Man" because he also competed in the mile, broad jump, mile-relay team, and cross-country. The school records he set remained unbroken for nearly a quarter-century. Born in Terry to Norwegian emigrants and raised on a ranch between Circle and Brockway, Ueland graduated from Brockway High School in 1935. After a life in agriculture and public service, he died in Butte in 2004.

Photo: Ole Ueland, second from left. The coach, right, is Harry Adams.

Browning

MARTIN "BUD" CONNELLY

RODEO

For 60 years—yes, 60—Connelly was a rodeo competitor, earning spots as a finalist in the National High School rodeo in 1951 and 1954. He is a 14-time Indian Rodeo Canadian Association champion and won NRA bareback, saddle bronc and all-around titles. In all, he's won 400 rodeo buckles and more than 20 saddles. He was still competing in his mid-70s. Later in his career, he was a renowned hazer aboard his horse "One-Eyed Sam." Connelly's persona earned him roles in such movies as *Hidalgo, Cheyenne* and *Appaloosa*. He has been inducted into the Montana Indian Athletic Hall of Fame, Montana Cowboy Hall of Fame and Western Heritage Center.

Brusett

JERRY COULTER

BASEBALL

A member of the only Jordan High basketball team to make it to the Class C state tournament until 2020, Coulter averaged better than 20 points per game in 1968. He also was the quarterback on the first Mustangs football team to defeat Wibaux. In 1968, Coulter set a District 4C high jump record by using something called the "Eastern roll"—a precursor to the Fosbury Flop. But Coulter's favorite sport was baseball, and he walked on at Montana State, which had offered him a football scholarship as a wide receiver. A member of the Brusett Yankees as a 12-year-old, Coulter once earned two victories in relief in the same day against Montana in 1971. After college, he focused on softball and played shortstop on an all-star team that defeated The King and His Court. Coulter pitched three years at MSU before the school dropped its baseball program.

Busby

MELBERT "MOKE" EAGLEFEATHERS

BASKETBALL

Considered the most colorful player on the 1971 Class C state championship Busby Eagles and a descendent of Chief Dull Knife, Eaglefeathers averaged more than 20 points per game in both the 1971 and '72 state tournaments. He was nicknamed "The Clown Prince of Basketball." As a child "Bird Chief" had open-heart surgery and a lung removed, and was told he'd never play sports, yet he did—learning basketball from his Northern Cheyenne grandfather using a taped-up sock. After high school, he attended the University of Nebraska for three years and played semi-pro ball. He later coached in Lame Deer before taking a job in Butte as director of the North American Indian Alliance, where he was appointed as an advisor to President Obama's Native American Cabinet. He was executive director of the NAIA when he died in 2016.

Butte

SONNY HOLLAND

FOOTBALL

In a town known for its toughness, Allyn "Sonny" Holland might've been the toughest of them all. He was a three-sport star for Butte High, playing center on the football team, then moved on to Montana State, where he was named captain as a freshman in 1956. Holland was a three-time All-American at center for the Bobcats, helping them to the 1956 NAIA national title and their first win in Missoula in 54 years. His No. 52 at MSU eventually was retired, he is widely considered "The Greatest Bobcat" and in a 1999 survey of Bobcat administrators by the *Bozeman Daily Chronicle* he was selected "MSU Athlete of the Century." Also a top heavyweight boxer at MSC, Holland signed with the Dallas Cowboys in 1960. He coached the Bobcats to the NCAA Division II national crown in 1976 and retired with the school's best winning percentage. A statue of Holland is outside of Bobcat Stadium and he is in the Montana Football Hall of Fame.

Capitol

BOB LASATER

FOOTBALL

Raised in the southeast corner of Montana along Tie Creek, Lasater was a four-sport star at Ekalaka in the early 1950s and led the Bulldogs to an undefeated football season in 1953, scoring seven TDs and 45 points in a 51-36 victory over Medicine Lake for the title. He also led Ekalaka to a perfect baseball season in 1954. Lasater continued his athletic career by playing three sports at Dickinson State in North Dakota, earning All-America honors as a football standout. Eventually he became an assistant basketball coach at DSC and the school's 13th head football coach, guiding the team from 1972-75. In 1981 he was enshrined into the Blue Hawk Hall of Fame. Lasater still lives in North Dakota.

Cardwell

KAILEE OLIVERSON

BASKETBALL/TRACK

Living in the center of a triangle of three schools near former NBC broadcaster Chet Huntley's birth town, Oliverson chose to attend Twin Bridges, where she was dominant in basketball, volleyball and track. Her favorite, though, was basketball and she was a rarity for Montana: A McDonald's All-American, in 2018. She was recruited to Nevada (Reno) and played as a freshman before returning north to continue her basketball and track career at Northern State in Aberdeen, South Dakota. In track, Oliverson won six Class C titles in the hurdles and relays, and she was second six more times, setting school records in the 100 and 300 hurdles.

Carter

LONES WIGGER JR.

RIFLE

A two-time Olympic gold medalist, Wigger—who attended high school in nearby Fort Benton—was described by *Gun Week* magazine as "by far the greatest shooter in history." He broke 29 world records, won 58 U.S. championships, and would've appeared in four Olympics had the U.S. not boycotted the 1980 games in Moscow. A three-time All-American at Montana State, he was a gold medalist in the 1964 and 1972 Olympics, and also won a silver. In 1996, he was honored as one of the U.S. Olympic Committee's 100 Golden Olympians and 12 years later was inducted in the United States Olympic Hall of Fame. Upon his death in December 2017 at age 80, the *New York Times* eulogized him as the "best ever." The range at the Olympic Training Center in Colorado Springs, Colorado, is named in his honor.

Cascade

HARRY CLARK

TRACK AND FIELD

To this day, no track athlete in Montana history has won more medals at a state meet than Clark, who owns 22. In the early 1980s, Clark set records in five Class B events and led Cascade to state titles in 1983 and '84. Of the 22 medals, 11 were gold. After high school, Clark started his collegiate career at Houston but eventually went on to become an All-American decathlete at Montana State, where he still holds the school record for points (7,633). When he retired from competition, he became the track and field coach first at Stanford High and then at Carroll College, where he's been in charge since 2013. Clark was inducted into the MHSA Hall of Fame in 2014 and MSU's Hall in 2018.

Centerville

PATRICE ANTHONY

CROSS COUNTRY

As a three-time state champion, Anthony is in select company with eight other girls in Montana history (four have won four titles). She took three consecutive crowns from 1982-84 and she remains second (12:00.6) and third (12:07.9) all-time for the two-mile run, staged from 1976-85. In addition, the 31 points Centerville scored in winning the Class C title in 1982 rank fifth all-time for low score at a state meet.

Charlo

STUART PERRY

FOOTBALL/BASKETBALL

It's difficult to say where Perry was more dominant, in football or basketball. On the gridiron he set career 8-Man records with 6,682 yards passing and 92 touchdowns from 1996-98. At the time, he ranked third and fourth in the nation among 8-Man schools in those categories. Perry was a first-team all-stater on both sides of the ball. In hoops, he scored 2,075 points, was a four-time first-team all-state Class C player and was the third western Montana player to surpass 2,000 points. He averaged 22 points per game in his career. Perry, who also threw the javelin, helped the Vikings to their first state basketball tournament in 21 years by scoring 41 points in the championship game of the Western C divisional in 1999.

Chester

CASEY FITZSIMMONS

FOOTBALL

The poster child for the small school, FitzSimmons rose from 8-Man football at Chester and the NAIA game at Carroll College to play for six years with the Detroit Lions of the NFL. He was an all-conference tight end four times at Carroll, NAIA and Frontier Conference Player of the Year finalist in 2003, a two-time NAIA All-American and helped lead the Saints to the national title in 2002—when he caught 79 passes for 971 yards and six TDs. At age 29, FitzSimmons retired from the NFL in 2010 after seven years and seven concussions. He played four positions at Chester, where he was a standout on the basketball court, too. FitzSimmons, now a cattle rancher outside of Helena, was inducted into the Montana Football Hall of Fame in 2018.

Chinook

BEN STROH

WRESTLING

A four-time Class B-C state champion, Stroh didn't just win on the mat—he dominated, winning 92 percent of his high school matches by fall. In doing so, he established a national record for consecutive pins, finishing his career at 101 with his fall in 39 seconds for title No. 4 in 2012. At 189 pounds, he is the heaviest four-time state champ in Montana history. By the time his high school career was over, he'd fashioned a 156-2 record, losing twice as a freshman. Stroh was no slouch on the football field, either, earning all-state honors and scoring six TDs in leading Chinook to the Class C state title in 2010. On the track, he was a standout in the 400, 800, discus and shot put. Stroh started his college wrestling career at Wyoming and qualified for the NCAA meet twice before transferring to MSU-Northern and winning an NAIA national championship at 184 pounds his senior season.

Choteau

FLINT RASMUSSEN

RODEO

Once a high school history and math teacher, Rasmussen—who is the first to insist he's not a great athlete—nevertheless evolved to become the most famous clown on the Professional Bull Riders circuit after years with the Professional Rodeo Cowboys Association, an achievement that requires a mix of athleticism and showmanship. At Choteau, he was an all-stater in football (quarterback) and track. Born in Havre, Rasmussen graduated from Montana Western and both taught and coached in high school in his native home. He worked his first rodeo in Superior in 1987 and eventually earned his first NFR berth in 1998. He was eight-time PRCA Clown of the Year, eight-time Wrangler National Finals Rodeo barrelman and Coors "Man in the Can" seven times. Rasmussen, who was inducted into the Pendleton Round-Up Hall of Fame in 2011 and the Ellensburg Rodeo Hall of Fame in 2019, recently left the arena to do a rodeo podcast and produce a show called "Outside The Barrel."

Churchill

BLYTHE HOMMES (HINTZ)

BASKETBALL

Still one of the top scorers in Manhattan Christian history, Hommes didn't slow down when she arrived at Montana State in 1993. By the time she was a senior, she averaged 18.9 points and 9.4 rebounds per game for the Bobcats, earning 1997 Big Sky Conference Player of the Year honors and a berth on the Kodak District VII All-America team. Hommes was inducted into MSU's Hall of Fame in 2007. Hommes wasn't just a basketball player. She led Manhattan Christian to the 1992 Class C state track and field title by scoring 48 of her team's 69 points, winning the 200, 400, 300 hurdles (state record) and triple jump, and finishing second in the 100 hurdles. A year later, she went two points better (50) and won five more events. Hommes also starred for the Eagles' volleyball team. She now lives in Lynden, Washington, where she is an assistant basketball coach for Lynden Christian.

Circle

DON SCHILLINGER

FOOTBALL

A quarterback and co-captain on the Wildcats' football team in 1964, Schillinger was a four-sport standout who also led Circle to the Class B state basketball championship in March 1965. He went on to play basketball and football at Carroll College before getting his degree at Montana. Schillinger etched his name in Montana lore, though, at Baker High School, where he spent 29 of his 37 years as a head coach. He retired in 2010 with 318 career victories, second only to Great Falls CMR's Jack Johnson (319) in state history, and never having a losing season. Under Schillinger's watch, the Spartans won six Class B state titles. Including an eight-year stint at Ekalaka (56-8 record), Schillinger won 27 conference titles and qualified for the playoffs 31 times, had 99 shutouts, won a state-record 37 consecutive road games and had 62 straight conference wins from 1997-2010. After retiring from coaching, he remained at Baker as superintendent.

Clancy

SHEILA GREEN (GERDING)

BASKETBALL

A standout at Jefferson High School down the road in Boulder, Green went on to even greater achievements at MSU-Northern, where she was a three-year starter on the most successful Northern Lights' programs in school history and graduated as the school's leading career scorer. Northern went to the NAIA national tournament all four years of her tenure, and she was all-Frontier Conference for three years—earning conference co-MVP honors and distinction as a Kodak All-American in 1992, when the Lights were ranked No. 1 nationally. Green immediately signed on as an assistant coach at MSU Billings, became an all-star playing professionally in New Zealand for a year, then returned to the States to coach. She coached at Minot State for 22 years before stepping down in 2017 as the winningest coach in school history (360-283). Green is now a K-12 counselor in Minot.

Clyde Park

BROCK PETERSON

FOOTBALL

Peterson's name is sprinkled all over the state 8-Man record books for his performances from 2013-16 for Shields Valley High. His 4,779 total yards rank seventh all time and his back-to-back 1,803 yards in 2016 and 1,539 in 2015 rank ninth and 10th. Peterson gained most of his yards on the ground, amassing 4,249 over his career, good for third all-time in the state. He once rushed for 382 in a single game. A standout in track as well, Peterson is continuing his football career as a running back at Rocky Mountain College. Off the field, Peterson was vice president of the Montana Business Professionals of America as a junior at Shields Valley.

Cohagen

BOBBY BROOKS (KRAMER)

RODEO

Bobby Brooks Kramer was a National Cowgirl Hall of Famer who lived and worked on a 150,000-acre ranch with her husband, Bud, a Montana Cowboy Hall of Fame inductee and uncle of NFL Hall of Famer Jerry Kramer, a Jordan native. In 1989, she was one of two women chosen for the Great Montana Centennial Cattle Drive. Brooks has six American Quarter Horse Association (AQHA) all-around championships to her name and is featured in the documentaries *I'll Ride That Horse* and *The Last Stronghold.* Brooks became a pilot to round up wayward horses on the family's vast ranch and later won air races. In 2000, she was inducted into the National Cowgirl Hall of Fame. A native of Terry, she died in 2005 at age 91.

Colstrip

CHRIS CURRIER

WRESTLING

A trail blazer in a prominent wrestling family, Currier laid the groundwork by winning four consecutive state championships—becoming only the eighth Montanan to do so at the time—and taking his fourth in 1994 at 130 pounds when the Colts were still in Class A. He didn't slow down in college, winning the 1999 NCAA Division II crown at 149 pounds for Southern Colorado. Currier was a Little Sullivan Award finalist that year. He also placed eighth in the 1994 national Greco-Roman tournament. Currier's brother Codey won two state titles and his nephews, Gage, Clayton, Jackson and Oden also are accomplished wrestlers; Clayton and Jackson followed their his uncle's footsteps by winning four state crowns.

Columbia Falls

MIKE LYNGSTAD

TRACK AND FIELD

A pole vault specialist in high school, Lyngstad became a legend in the javelin by winning three Big Sky Conference championships at Montana in the late 1960s, setting a conference record first with 238-0 1/2 in 1968 and breaking it with 245-2 in 1969—a mark that has yet to be broken. In 1969 he set the Griz record with a toss of 253-9, at the time the third farthest in the nation, and he is still considered the greatest javelin thrower in conference history. Lyngstad also played a year of football for the Griz before going into the military, learning the art of throwing—and coaching—the javelin from Scandanavians. After leaving UM, he was with the U.S. Olympic Track & Field team. Lyngstad retired from coaching the javelin at Columbia Falls in 2020 and was eventually planning to move to Hamilton.

Columbus

DWAN EDWARDS

FOOTBALL

A three-sport athlete and senior class president for the Cougars, Edwards went on to a high-profile career in college at Oregon State and in the NFL with three teams as a defensive tackle. He was a two-time all-Pac-10 pick and was drafted in the second round by the Baltimore Ravens before finishing his career with a Super Bowl appearance with the Carolina Panthers in 2016. Edwards was co-MVP on Oregon State's 2003 team and a two-time all-stater at Columbus. In high school, Edwards was a high-scoring forward in basketball for the Cougars, averaging over 20 points per game in 1999. He is retired from the game today and was inducted into the Montana Football Hall of Fame in 2016. Edwards lives in Charlotte, North Carolina.

Conrad

LONI PERKINS (JUDISCH)

TRACK AND FIELD

A sprinter and jumper, Perkins is tied with Toni Quenell of Geraldine for most medals won at state meets with 24, including 13 golds. As a junior in 2002, she became the first girl and second Montana athlete ever to win seven golds in a state meet, winning the long jump, high jump, 100, 200 and 400 individually while anchoring Conrad's first-place 400 and 1,600 relay teams. Perkins won four medals each in the 200, 400 and 1,600-meter relay, took three in the 400 relay and for good measure won two in the 100 and long jump and another in the triple jump from 2000-03. Perkins, who also competed in volleyball and basketball, still owns state records in the 200 and 400 set in 2003. Perkins went on to compete in track at Montana, where she was a four-time Big Sky champion in the 400 and won eight conference titles overall. Today she's a cattle rancher and lifestyle photographer in Montana's Golden Triangle.

Corvallis

LORNA GRIFFIN

TRACK AND FIELD

As a high schooler raised on a dairy farm in the Bitterroot Valley, Griffin was a standout in both the discus and shot put—setting a state record in the shot. But her forte was the discus, where she made the U.S. Olympic team in 1980 and 1988, becoming the first U.S. woman to throw over 200 feet in the process. Griffin also made the Olympics in the discus AND shot in 1984, and she won silver medals in the 1983 Pan American Games in both events. For a brief time in 1983, she held the American discus mark. A talented weightlifter as well, in 1984 Griffin won the Best Lifter Award at the National Women's Weightlifting Championships. After starting collegiately at Flathead Valley Community College, she attended Seattle Pacific, where she set a discus record that still stands. Now a resident of Huntington Beach, California, Griffin was inducted into Seattle Pacific's Hall of Fame in 2005.

Crow Agency

LARRY PRETTY WEASEL

BASKETBALL

Though only 5-foot-10, Pretty Weasel was a mercurial player for Hardin in the 1950s, averaging 32 points a game during the 1957 state tournament. That year, he scored 48 points in the third-place game—a record that stood for 27 years—and for an encore put up 50 in the East-West Shrine All-Star Game. Pretty Weasel was chosen Montana's top high school athlete overall in 1957 after setting the state's single-season scoring record with 712 points. His 465 points in conference action that year, despite double- and triple-teams, also set a record for Class A and AA. Recruited by several major colleges, he was leading the nation in field goal percentage as a freshman at Rocky Mountain College when he dropped out of school midseason. Nicknamed "The Hardin Flash," Pretty Weasel was inducted into the Montana Indian Athletic Hall of Fame in its inaugural class in 2007. He still lives in Crow Agency and has watched three great-grandchildren win state basketball titles for Hardin and Lodge Grass.

Culbertson

TERRY FALCON

FOOTBALL

A three-sport star with the Cowboys, Falcon made his name in football—playing college ball at Minot State and Montana before embarking on a career as an offensive lineman in the NFL and USFL. A two-time all-conference left guard with the Griz, Falcon was an eighth-round draft choice of the New England Patriots in 1978. He also played two years with the New York Giants and another year with Arizona of the USFL. At Culbertson, Falcon set a district record in the shot put and was also a champion in the discus. He was a standout in basketball, too, once scoring 24 points and grabbing 27 rebounds in a game as a center. After retiring from pro football, Falcon eventually became head football coach at Missoula Loyola in the early 2000s before moving to Poplar to become a vice principal.

Photo: Terry Falcon, No. 60

Custer

STEVE AND JEFF KELLER

BASKETBALL

It's hard to distinguish the Keller boys, whose on-court exploits in back-to-back careers dominate the Custer record books. Steve ranks ninth and Jeff 10th all-time in Montana career scoring, with 2,206 and 2,181 points. Jeff ranks fourth for career field goals made with 794 and eighth for points in a season with 755, and Steve is eighth with 22 baskets made in a single game. And they rank Nos. 1 and 3 in state history in free throws made in a career, Steve with 617 and Jeff at 467; Steve's 224 in 1972-73 remain a record for season and the 24 made in a game also is tops all time in the state. Steve now coaches the men's basketball team at Providence.

Photo: Jeff Keller, No. 15

Cut Bank

DON WETZEL SR.

BASKETBALL

A three-time Class B all-state selection in high school, Wetzel was the first Native American to play NCAA Division I basketball for four years, earning all-Big Sky honors for the Montana Griz during a career that spanned 1967-71. He was team MVP his senior year. A year after leading Cut Bank to the 1966 state basketball title, Wetzel was an All-American. He also was a state champion in the low hurdles and high jump in track, was all-state as a quarterback in football, and played baseball. After finishing his career at Montana, he coached the freshman team one year at UM under the legendary Jud Heathcote before coaching at Browning for eight—winning the 1980 Class A state title—and eventually taking the reins at Helena High. Wetzel was inducted into the MHSA Hall of Fame in 2002 and is a co-founder of the Montana Indian Athletic Hall of Fame, into which he was inducted in 2011. He lives in Helena.

Dagmar

BRUCE SMITH

BASKETBALL

A 6-foot-10 center, Smith was a scoring machine for Medicine Lake in the early 1970s, earning MVP honors at the 1972 state Class B tournament and all-state honors as a senior. A native of Williston, North Dakota, Smith was a Scholastic Coach's Top 100 player in the nation his final two years with the Honkers. After high school, Smith played for Montana State, securing 23 rebounds in a game with the freshman team and eventually starting at center as a junior and senior. He played professionally for a year in France before returning to MSU to earn a master's degree in business administration and become an extension agent back home in eastern Montana, where he raised sheep. Smith returned to school at Cal Poly-San Luis Obispo in 1987, lived briefly in Illinois and Idaho, and returned to Montana as an extension agent in Twin Bridges before moving to Glendive in a similar role. He died of cancer in 2019 at age 63 in Fallon.

Darby

TODD BERRY

WRESTLING

A three-time state champion (1978-80), Berry managed to emerge from his small town in the Bitterroot Valley to earn *USA Today* All-American honors and qualified for the Olympic Trials in 1980 as a 17-year-old. Upon his graduation from Darby, he'd accumulated more victories than any wrestler in state history. Along the way, he also won the 1980 state Class B-C pole vault championship. After wrestling in high school at 126 and 138 pounds and finishing with what was then a state-record 117 victories, he went on to compete for North Idaho College in Coeur d'Alene, Idaho, before working in the mining industry in Idaho and then as a lineman for Northwestern Energy. Berry died of cancer in 2012 at age 50.

Deer Lodge

JOE BIGNELL

FOOTBALL

With a salute to NBA playing star and coaching legend Phil Jackson, who was born in Deer Lodge, the nod goes to Bignell, an all-stater in football and basketball in the 1970s for the Wardens. In basketball, he scored more than 1,500 points for his career and poured in a school-record 46 points in one game. But it was as a tight end in football that he excelled most, earning scholarship offers from four Pac-10 schools. At Montana State, he was an honorable mention All-American in 1984 while helping the Bobcats to their third national championship. He ranked 12th nationally with more than 1,000 yards in receptions in '84, catching 10 passes and two TDs in MSU's title-game win over Louisiana Tech. In 2008, he was inducted into MSU's Hall of Fame.

Denton

KATIE EDWARDS

BASKETBALL

Were it not for Kayla Lambert, Edwards would sit atop Montana's career scoring list for girls basketball. From 1998-2001, she scored 2,650 points while playing for Denton and Lewistown high schools. She ranks fourth and fifth in single-season scoring, with 705 and 694 points. For her career, she averaged 26.8 points, putting her third in state history, and in 2001 led Lewistown to the Class A state title. As a freshman, she hit 62 consecutive free throws and likely has made more than any player in state history. Per the MHSA record books, her 82.4% success rate at the line ranks No. 1 in state history. At Montana from 2001-06, Edwards set the school record for 3-pointers with 236, tops for a career in the Big Sky Conference at the time and still fourth, and she was all-conference twice. Edwards, who set a Big Sky single-game record with nine 3-pointers, ranks sixth in career scoring for the Lady Griz with 1,400 points.

Dillon

MANDI CARVER

BASKETBALL

Carver excelled in volleyball and track, but she made her name in basketball in high school, college and as a coach. She was first-team all-state for three years and set eight school records, including most field goals made in a career (440) and most rebounds (716) as Dillon won the Class A state title in 1995 and finished second twice after that. Carver also was first-team all-state in volleyball and was all-state three times in track. She played collegiately at Idaho State, where she set five school records, was 2001 Big Sky Conference Player of the Year and eventually was honored as one of the league's top 25 players of all time. Carver led the nation in rebounding in 2001-02 and left ISU as the school's career leading scorer, rebounder and shot blocker. In 2002, she signed as a free agent with the Detroit Shock of the WNBA and then played overseas professionally for seven years with nine teams, earning MVP honors in the Swiss League and Latvian League as well as all-star status in Greece. Upon retiring, Carver became a college coach, first at Cal State-Bakersfield and then at San Jose State. Since 2016, she has been associate head women's coach and recruiting coordinator at Fresno State.

Dixon

JIM CLAIRMONT

FOOTBALL

Clairmont broke a Class C record in the javelin in 1962 with a heave of 193-4 1/2, but he excelled as much on the football field as he did in track and field, and he was a standout high school basketball player as well. At Western Montana, he qualified for NAIA nationals for four consecutive years in the javelin, eventually setting a national record with a throw of 225-4. In football, Clairmont was a two-time Frontier Conference defensive lineman of the year and was NAIA District V lineman of the year in 1967. Clairmont, who has taught biological science for more than two decades in Ronan, was inducted into Montana Western's Hall of Fame in 1990.

Dodson

LYLE COCHRAN

RODEO

A registered Assiniboine from the Fort Belknap Reservation, Cochran competed in rodeo for well over 50 years and in 1976 was the Indian National Finals Rodeo's first national champion. In all, he won 47 saddles during his illustrious career. A tie-down roper, Cochran was the Montana Pro Rodeo Circuit champion in 1978 and 1980. He won the Montana Pro Rodeo all-around average title in 1986. Cochran won hundreds of buckles. He was enshrined in the Indian National Finals Rodeo Hall of Fame in 2014 and the Montana Indian Athletic Hall of Fame in 2016.

Drummond

CHASE REYNOLDS

FOOTBALL

In four years playing 8-Man football for Drummond, Reynolds amassed a state-record 5,261 rushing yards and was a four-time all-state selection, winning three state titles in the process. He was a dynamo on the track as well, winning the state long jump crown and finishing second in the triple jump in 2004. At Montana in 2008, he set a single-season record with 22 touchdowns, a mark he equaled a year later. As a senior, Reynolds was a finalist for the Walter Payton Award. He went undrafted but played six years in the NFL, signing first with the Seattle Seahawks but playing mostly with the St. Louis/Los Angeles Rams on special teams. Upon retiring, he returned to Missoula, where he sells real estate and lost a close race for a state Senate seat in 2018.

Dutton

NATE ODDEN

FOOTBALL

Odden did it all for Dutton in the early 1980s—earning all-state honors in football, basketball and track. In 1983 he set a Class C state record in the 300 hurdles, and he was also state champion in the 100 dash and 110 hurdles. In basketball, he was all-conference and it wasn't unusual to see more than 20 points by his name in the box score. But football was his favorite sport and it's where Odden shined. He was quarterback, linebacker, punter and kicker for a high-powered Dutton offense, and was considered by many to be the top player in Class C. Odden took his football prowess to Montana, eventually starting as a cornerback before moving to safety and then linebacker. After college, Odden settled down in Missoula and now lives in Ketchikan, Alaska.

East Glacier

SIMARRON SCHILDT (ROBERTSON)

BASKETBALL

The high school uniform said Browning, but Schildt grew up on the fringes of Glacier National Park and went on to become a starting forward at Montana, where she was the second Native American to play for the Griz—after Malia Kipp, also of Browning. A 4.0 student and high school valedictorian, Schildt led the Indians to their only Class A state basketball championship in 1996, averaging better than 17 points and 11 rebounds a game. She was inducted into the Montana Indian Athletic Hall of Fame in 2018. Schildt is back on the Blackfeet Reservation near East Glacier, where she owns a company that designs and makes dreamcatchers.

East Helena

BRIAN SCHWEYEN

TRACK AND FIELD

A solid basketball player at Helena High, Schweyen was a trail blazer in track and field, where he set the school record of 6-10 in the high jump—a mark that lasted 31 years. And Schweyen was just beginning: At Montana State, he was the first man in the world to high jump 7 feet and pole vault 17 feet on the same day, an achievement he would accomplish three more times. He won four of his six Big Sky championships in the high jump, twice earning All-America honors. After college, Schweyen became a decathlete, ranking as high as eighth nationally. The head track coach at Montana from 2008-2020, he is in the Hall of Fame at both MSU and Helena High.

Edgar

PARKER BREDING

RODEO

A starting guard on the Joliet High basketball team, Breding comes with solid bull-riding DNA, thanks to his father, Scott, a five-time NFR qualifier. Parker has won the RAM National Circuit Finals Rodeo title three times—only the second cowboy, along with Hall of Famer Cody Custer, to achieve the feat. He has qualified for the NFR three times himself, and was ranked as high as fourth in the world standings in 2018. Breding was a two-time Montana bull riding champ as well. He was battling knee injuries in 2019 and contemplating his future in the sport in early 2020.

Ekalaka

PAT HANSEN

FOOTBALL

From the remote southeast corner of the state, Hansen was an all-stater for the Bulldogs, starting for four consecutive years on both sides of the ball. He then played collegiately at Montana Tech, where he rushed for more than 1,000 yards for four consecutive seasons—ranking third in the nation in 2011. Hansen ran for 178 yards and five TDs in his first game as a freshman and wound up as team MVP after rushing for 1,400 yards. As a sophomore he led the team in scoring and led the Frontier Conference in rushing. In his final game in 2014, Hansen passed Don Heater's 43-year-old career rushing mark with 4,486 yards. Today, he is a mining engineer living in Laurel.

Ennis

JESSIE ROYER

MUSHER

A ranch girl from the get-go, Royer has parlayed her love of huskies into a noteworthy career as a musher. She bought her first sled dogs at age 15 and two years later became the youngest winner of Montana's Race to the Sky. She was Rookie of the Year at the Iditarod Trail Sled Dog Race in Alaska in 2001 and has finished as high as third overall twice (2019 and 2020), ranking her as one of the top female mushers of all time. She has earned Champion Status at the Iditarod seven times for finishing in the top 10 and overall has won more than $400,000 in Alaska's Super Bowl. In 2017, she finished eighth in the Yukon Quest. Royer splits her time between homes at Seeley Lake and Fairbanks, Alaska.

Eureka

SHANNON BUTLER

TRACK AND FIELD

One of the greatest distance runners Montana has ever produced, Butler won two NCAA championships and 12 Big Sky Conference titles while running for Montana State. Among the Big Sky's 50 greatest male athletes, Butler ranks fourth. After starting his collegiate career at Auburn, he returned home and won the Big Sky's cross country titles in 1989 and '90, and was NCAA Mountain Regional champion in '90 before finishing second at the NCAA Championships in 1990. In 1991, Butler was the Big Sky's winner in the 1,500, 5,000 and 10,000 meters—the first athlete to accomplish that trifecta—and also finished third in the 3,000 at the NCAA Indoor Championships in '91. In 2001, he was inducted into the MSU Hall of Fame. After college, Butler won the 10,000 meters at the USA Track and Field national championships in New York while wearing his MSU uniform. He still holds the all-class three-mile high school cross country record, set while running for Eureka in 1985. After retiring, he moved to Darby, where he works for a property management firm out of Missoula.

Fairfield

JILL BARTA

BASKETBALL

Without a doubt, Barta is one of the top female basketball players in Montana history, illuminated by her 104-0 record from 2010-14 at Class B Fairfield, where she also was a standout in volleyball. She averaged 23 points and eight rebounds a game as a senior, earning MVP honors in the state tournament. She scored 41 points and had 18 rebounds in Fairfield's two-overtime win over Malta, scoring the Eagles' final 21 points. After her dominating high school career, Barta starred at Gonzaga, where she was the team's leading scorer for three seasons before leaving after her junior year as the fourth-leading scorer in school history (1,620 points). In 2018, Barta was the West Coast Conference Player of the Year, a Cheryl Miller Award finalist as one of the best small forwards in the nation, and a Region 5 All-American. She still holds Gonzaga's career record for free-throw percentage (87.6). Barta was drafted by Las Vegas of the WNBA and had a preseason stint with the Minnesota Lynx, then played professionally for Budocnost in Montenegro in 2019.

Fairview

MARTI KINZLER

BASKETBALL

Only one player can say they're first in any category, and when it comes to scoring 2,000 points for a career Kinzler surpassed the barrier first. She finished her Fairview high school career in 1986 with 2,053 points and earned All-America honors in the process. Kinzler was all-state all four of her years with the Warriors and made all-state in volleyball as well. She didn't slow down at Montana, where she was all-conference and finished among the program's top 20 leaders in six categories. Kinzler was inducted into the MHSA Athletes Hall of Fame in 1996. Now Marti Kinzler-Vining, she lives in Great Falls and has a daughter, Haley, who played basketball at UM.

Fishtail

BUCK REINER

RODEO

An accomplished saddle bronc rider on the PRCA, Reiner had a big run in 2003 after taking four years off from the circuit. In a three-week span, he won rodeos in Red Lodge and two more in Canada. In between, the Colorado State graduate was a fiber-optics inspector in Washington. Reiner owns a trucking company in Fishtail.

Flaxville

KEVIN HATFIELD

BASKETBALL

For several years in the heady '70s, the tiny little town in northeastern Montana enjoyed glory in hoops, led by the towering 6-foot-7 Hatfield. As a freshman in 1976, Hatfield earned MVP honors in the state tournament. He repeated the feat three years later as a senior, scoring 24 points in the state title game against neighboring Peerless to give the Cards their second Class C crown. Hatfield still ranks third all-time in state history in career rebounds with 1,320. He was a star discus thrower as well, breaking a 17-year-old state record in 1979. Hatfield played two years of college basketball at Westmont College in California before transferring to Minot State. He lives in Minot.

Florence

JIM TYACK

BASEBALL

The son of a Butte copper miner, Tyack was born in Florence in 1911 and spent the first eight years of his youth there. The family eventually moved to Bakersfield, California, where he was a four-sport high school star and made a name for himself first at Fresno State and then at Bakersfield College, where he lettered in four sports. Tyack kicked around the minor leagues for many years before pitching one season in the major leagues as a 32-year-old rookie, with the Philadelphia Phillies in 1943. He later was a player-manager for the Pocatello (Idaho) Cardinals in the Pioneer League. Back home in Bakersfield, Tyack owned a tire distributorship. He was inducted into the Kern County (California) Hall of Fame in 1974 and an award in his name is given out each year to the top high school athlete in the county. He died in 1995 after suffering a heart attack.

Forsyth

THE WEBER BROTHERS

WRESTLING

The Weber family is synonymous with wrestling success, winning 17 state championships between the five brothers (Brandon 3, Luke 4, Michael 4, Matt 4 and Nathan 2). Luke Weber won four state championships for Forsyth from 2013-16 before earning a wrestling scholarship to Nebraska, where he was 19-6 as a redshirt freshman. In 2016, he won a national championship in the 145-pound division at the National High School Coaches Association meet. At Forsyth, he was 212-5 with 174 pins for his career, setting state records in both categories and losing only one match in his final three seasons. Weber, whose 58 wins in 2014 are a state record, also was a three-time all-stater in football. Michael Weber also was a four-time state B-C champion for the Dogies. In 2017, he won a wrestling triple crown, taking first place at the High School Coaches Association Nationals, USAW Folkstyle Nationals and the Reno Worlds. Matt also was a four-time state champ and a medal winner for MSU-Northern. Nathan, who also won a state title in track, was a B-C state champ and also wrestled in college for the Lights. The oldest, Brandon, was a three-time state champion and won an NAIA national crown for MSU-Northern in 2017.

Photo: Matt Weber

Fort Belknap

JIMMY COLE

RODEO

A heeler, Cole won two Montana PRCA crowns (1997 and 1999) working with header Sam Bird and also won two Indian National Finals Rodeos with Bird's nephew Dustin Bird. Cole, who also called Harlem his home, was the Northern Plains Indian Rodeo Association year-end champion in 2005.

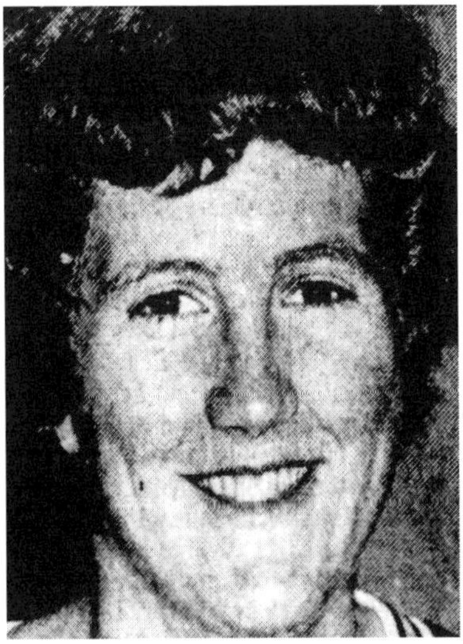

Fort Benton

DENISE CURRY

BASKETBALL

Yes, it's true—one of the greatest female basketball players in American history spent her formative youth in Fort Benton, leaving Montana in 1966. After moving to Chico and then Davis, California, for high school, Curry signed with UCLA, where she was a three-time All-American and set 14 school records, graduating as the all-time leading scorer and rebounder. She won gold medals at the 1979 Pan American Games, 1981 World University Games and 1984 Olympics, and was on the Olympic team in 1980 when the U.S boycotted the Moscow Games. In 1981, Curry was the USA Basketball Female Athlete of the Year. Curry, whose father, Les, led the league in scoring three times for Montana State in the early '50s and then coached at several Montana high schools, won a national championship playing professionally in France. She was the head coach at Cal State-Fullerton and an assistant at California, with the San Jose Lasers of the Women's American Basketball League and finally at Long Beach State, retiring in 2009. In 1997 she was the 11th female enshrined in the Naismith Basketball Hall of Fame. Curry also is in the UCLA and Women's Basketball halls of fame, the latter in its inaugural class; her No. 12 jersey was one of the first four retired by UCLA (Ann Meyers, Kareem Abdul-Jabbar and Bill Walton). She is retired and living in Los Angeles.

Fort Keogh

VAL GLYNN

BASEBALL

One of the top all-round athletes in Montana State history, Glynn spent his early years along the banks of the Yellowstone River before his family moved to Utah. He arrived in Bozeman as a freshman in 1923 and proceeded to earn all-conference honors in football and basketball. But it was baseball where he was best, ultimately taking him to a career pitching for San Francisco and Salt Lake City of the Pacific Coast League and the Washington Senators in the late 1920s and early 1930s. Glynn earned 11 letters at MSC, falling shy of 12 only because freshmen couldn't play football. He later became MSU's Dean of Men for 17 years. A member of the Class of '28, Glynn was inducted into MSU's Hall of Fame as an athlete and administrator in 1987. He died in 1992 in Billings.

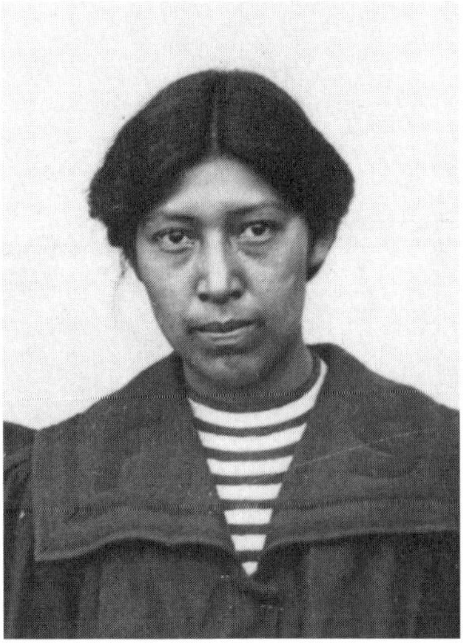

Fort Shaw

MINNIE BURTON

BASKETBALL

A Lemhi Shoshone who came to the Fort Shaw Indian Boarding School from Fort Hall, Idaho, Burton was the star player and fan favorite on the girls basketball team that was declared world champions after routing all comers at the 1904 St. Louis World's Fair. Burton was a guard and forward on a team that trounced Montana State 22-0 and Montana 25-1 before continuing its hot streak in St. Louis. They whipped St. Louis High 25-2 and twice beat the Missouri All-Stars badly, earning the crown after the second win. Burton's popularity was reflected in crowds chanting "Shoot, Minnie, Shoot, Shoot!" whenever she touched the ball. The team also won an anticlimactic world championship the next year in Portland, Oregon. After that, Burton became a seamstress and kindergarten teacher on the Lemhi Reservation in Idaho. She died in childbirth at age 30.

Frazer

MYA FOURSTAR

BASKETBALL

The youngest athlete on our list, Fourstar made headlines regionally and eventually nationally when she scored 50 points in a varsity high school basketball game—as an eighth grader. Fourstar's story and dreams of a basketball career were chronicled by *The Washington Post* in 2018. In her junior year after transferring to Wolf Point, she helped her team to the Class B state title and then followed up in the spring with a state high jump crown. Fourstar completed her high school career at Wolf Point in March 2020. She started her college basketball career at United Tribes Technical College in Bismarck, North Dakota, but returned home shortly after enrolling to be with family during the COVID-19 pandemic.

Frenchtown

MORGAN RAY

SOFTBALL

One of the most dominant pitchers in Montana history, Ray was a three-time Gatorade Player of the Year and first-team All-American while pitching the Broncs to three consecutive Class A titles (2013-15). In the process, she threw 10 no-hitters and one perfect game en route to fashioning a 0.32 earned-run average and holding opponents to a .114 cumulative batting average. She recently finished a decorated career at Ohio State, where she won 18 games and was second-team all-Midwest in 2018 and second-team all-Big Ten in 2019. Ray played professionally for a year in Europe, pitching the Kunovice Snails team to a bronze medal in the Czech Republic national tournament. A volleyball standout as well, Ray ranks 10th all-time in the state in career kills with 1,188 and eighth in blocks with 360.

Froid

TERRY ERICKSON

BASKETBALL

A terrific all-round athlete, Erickson starred in football, basketball and track in the late 1980s and early 1990s. He was an all-star receiver for the Froid-Medicine Lake co-op in football, was one of the team's top scorers in basketball, and was accomplished in track as a pole vaulter as well, winning the Eastern 2C title in 1991. In basketball, he was first-team all-conference in 1991.

Fromberg

DEB GREENOUGH

RODEO

A graduate of Fromberg High and a member of one of Montana's two most famous rodeo families—"The Riding Greenoughs"—Deb qualified for the National Finals Rodeo for 13 consecutive years from 1988-2000 and is tied for fifth-most NFR qualifications in PRCA history. His 15 go-round NFR wins also rank fifth all-time. Greenough won the NFR average title in 1992 and was world bareback champ a year later. He won three National Circuit Finals Rodeo bareback crowns, won more than $1.2 million for his career, and was the second bareback rider from Montana to be inducted into the ProRodeo Hall of Fame (2018).

Gardiner

HANNAH DEAN

BASKETBALL

Between the two sports, it was difficult to tell where Dean was better—though she chose basketball over volleyball for her collegiate career at Carroll. She was all-state and a three-time Class C state champion in volleyball at Gardiner but also was all-state and led the Bruins to their first-ever crown in hoops. At Carroll, Dean earned second-team All-America honors in 2018 and her jersey was chosen to hang in the Women's Basketball Hall of Fame Ring of Honor in Knoxville, Tennessee, to commemorate her exceptional season. In her senior season, she surpassed 1,000 points for her career. And after her collegiate basketball career ended, she joined the Saints' volleyball team.

Geraldine

DAREN AND KEVIN ENGELLANT

BASKETBALL

The Engellant brothers were high-scoring players for Geraldine and continued their prowess in college—Daren at the University of Montana, where he was a three-time all-Big Sky selection and scored 1,224 points with 874 rebounds over his career, and Kevin at Montana Western, where he amassed 1,423 points and wound up in the school's Hall of Fame. Daren ranks fifth in state history in rebounds (1,174) field goal percentage (63.2). Kevin, who retired as the winningest women's basketball coach in Montana Western history, ranks sixth in 3-point shots, seventh in rebounds and eighth in free throws made.

Geyser

RYAN MAPSTON

RODEO

One of the state's most accomplished saddle bronc riders, in the late 1990s and early 2000s Mapston was consistently among the leaders in the Wrangler Million Dollar Tour standings. He finished second in the world once and third twice in overall points. Despite having to compete against saddle bronc legend Dan Mortensen, he was the year-end champion in 1997 and '98 on the Montana Pro Rodeo Circuit and was average champion three times. A native of Arlee, Mapston moved to Geyser early in his rodeo career. In 2012, the 10-time National Finals Rodeo qualifier started the Ryan Mapston Bucking Horse Futurity and Ranch Rodeo in Belt. In December 2019, Mapston was inducted into the Montana Pro Rodeo Hall and Wall of Fame in the Rodeo Legends category.

Gildford

TRAVIS STEHMAN

CROSS COUNTRY

Stehman excelled in many sports, but he was at his best at running. He led Kremlin-Gildford to three consecutive Class C state cross country crowns and helped the Kougars repeat the feat in track and field. A twin, Stehman was the individual state cross country and 3,200-meter champion from 1996-98, remains one of only four athletes to win three crowns and still holds the Class C mark of 14:55.0 set in 1998. Stehman's prowess took him to the distance running capital of the world for track and cross country: the University of Oregon. After cutting his time at Oregon short, Stehman returned to the family farm, where he died at age 30 in 2011—12 years after the death of his twin brother, Trevor.

Glasgow

STEVE REEVES

BODYBUILDING

Born in Glasgow, Reeves had an illustrious bodybuilding career during which former Mr. Olympia Larry Scott described him as, "The best-looking, best-built man God has ever created." Reeves was at various times Mr. America (1947), Mr. World (1948) and Mr. Universe ('48 & '50). His ripped physique earned him the lead role for the 1958 movie *Hercules*. He later turned down the part that went to Clint Eastwood in *A Fistful of Dollars* and reportedly also rejected an overture to play James Bond in *Dr. No*. Reeves was born just north of Glasgow and spent part of his youth in Helena before moving to Oakland, California. He died of cancer in 2000; his ashes were scattered on a cousin's ranch in the Big Snowy Mountains near Lewistown and the rest were buried in the Scobey cemetery next to his grave of his father, Lester.

Glen

TIM GARRISON

RODEO

The 1989 national steer wrestling champion for Western Montana College, Garrison also was an NFR qualifier in the event. His national title for Western was the school's first ever in rodeo; he placed ninth in the all-around that year. In 1997, he was the year-end Montana Pro Rodeo Circuit Finals all-around champion. Also a standout calf roper, Garrison was inducted into the Montana Western Hall of Fame in 2001.

Glendive

MIKE PERSON

FOOTBALL

In twice earning lineman of the year and all-state honors for the Red Devils, Person—who also won two state discus championships—was just beginning to show his football wares. At Montana State, he started 35 consecutive games on the line for an offensive juggernaut. Person was a first-team All-American as a senior in 2010 and was drafted in the seventh round by the San Francisco 49ers on the same day he was announced as Montana's AAU Little Sullivan Award winner. An avid fly fisherman from his days at MSU, Person started for the 49ers in the Super Bowl against Kansas City in February 2020. He was released by San Francisco—his eighth stop in the league—shortly after and retired from the game in the summer of 2020.

Grass Range

MARY LOU MATOVICH (STULC)

BASKETBALL

Despite averaging 21 points, 15 rebounds and 5 assists per game over her four-year high school career in Grass Range, Matovich never envisioned the success transferring to college. But it did. In the late 1980s, Matovich was a standout guard for Rocky Mountain College, earning first-team all-Frontier Conference honors by her sophomore season and leading the Battlin' Bears to the 1988 NAIA national tournament. Matovich, who learned to shoot in the hayloft of the family barn, was a two-time first-team all-state selection, earned honorable mention as a freshman and sophomore, and was chosen to the All-*USA Today* girls honorable mention team with six other players in 1986. Matovich also was one of the top discus and javelin throwers in Grass Range's district. She lives on a ranch outside of Winifred.

Great Falls

DAVE DICKENSON

FOOTBALL

Often referred to as "The Legend of the Fall" and "Super Dave", Dickenson was a three-sport standout and led Great Falls to two state football championships. He played collegiately at Montana, leading the Grizzlies to the 1995 Division I-AA national title while earning the Walter Payton Award as the classification's top offensive player. After college, Dickenson was chosen Most Outstanding player in the CFL with the Calgary Stampeders and also spent two seasons with the San Diego Chargers of the NFL. Since 2009, he has been one of the CFLs top coaches, earning coach of the year honors in 2016. His No. 15 was retired at CMR and he's in the CFL Hall of Fame. Dickenson was ranked 12th on *Sports Illustrated*'s list of top 50 athletes from Montana—but survey anyone in Missoula and Great Falls, and chances are he'll rank No. 1.

Greycliff

RONNIE HALVERSON

FOOTBALL

Halversen made his first splash in goat tying and steer riding as a middle-schooler before moving on to become a four-sport athlete at Big Timber in the late 1980s. Halversen would win a high school steer riding state championship in 1986. Halversen was all-state in football and track, and also played basketball for the Herders. A member of a prominent ranching family, Halverson kept active as a member of the Montana Running Ranchers—a group from around the state that participates in long relay races while promoting the cattle industry.

Hall

JESS MARTIN

FOOTBALL

A cog in the Drummond football dynasty, Martin was an all-conference running back in 1987. In track, he was the Class C pole vault champion in 1987 and 1988, and finished fifth and fourth in the long jump. For 21 years, Martin shared the district long-jump record. He also was a top sprinter. After his high school career, Martin played football and turned to rodeo, becoming a saddle bronc champion at Western Montana College. Putting down roots in Dillon, he went on to win championships on the professional rodeo circuit. Martin made the first of three consecutive National Finals Rodeo appearances in 1996, finished third a year later behind Montanans Dan Mortensen and Ryan Mapston, and returned in 1998. After a run of injuries, he qualified again for the NFR in 2002. He also was the Montana Professional Rodeo Finals champion in 1999 and 2000, and set a record with an 88-point ride in 2001.

Hamilton

JODI ROBINSON

TENNIS

From 1987-90, Robinson established a record that can never be broken—only matched. She won four consecutive singles titles—three in Class A-B-C and one in Class A—to become the first Montana player to achieve the feat. She finished her varsity career with a 62-0 singles record and lost only one set in four years, doing so despite suffering a severe knee injury in basketball her senior season. Her feat earned her recognition in *Sports Illustrated*'s Faces in the Crowd. Robinson, also a standout guard on the Broncs' basketball team, was their No. 2 scorer as a senior. She played four years of tennis at Washington State, where she and Sheetal Khanna went 19-2 in 1994-95 to set the school doubles record for career winning percentage and set a single-season mark by going 11-1 in 1994.

Hardin

KROY BIERMANN

FOOTBALL

A three-sport star at Hardin, Biermann excelled as a linebacker in football, twice earning first-team all-state honors before matriculating at Montana. He won Big Sky Conference Defensive MVP honors and was UM's first Buck Buchanan Award winner in 2007. His 32 sacks are second most in school history. Biermann spent eight years with the Atlanta Falcons of the NFL, his career ending in 2016 after a brief stint with Buffalo. He also was an Eastern A champion and state runner-up at 215 pounds in wrestling, and he was a hurdler and jumper for the track team in high school. His wife, Kim Dolciak, who he met on the set of the Dancing Stars of Atlanta charity event, was a star on Bravo's *Real Housewives of Atlanta*. Today, Biermann is mostly a stay-at-home dad who champions his wife's projects.

Harlem

RICK HAS THE PIPE

TRACK AND FIELD

An all-star football player and talented basketball player as well, the Seattle-born Has The Pipe etched his name in Montana lore as a runner, breaking records in numerous events—most notably the 880 meters, where his time of 1:57.2 in 1962 set a state record. He is considered the finest runner in Harlem's history. After high school, Has The Pipe accepted a scholarship to run track and also play basketball at Oklahoma City University. He was co-captain of the OCU cross country team as a freshman in 1963 and eventually set school records in the 880 and mile. He was inducted into the Montana Indian Athletic Hall of Fame in 2014. Has The Pipe, who also played many years in Helena's city softball leagues, died in 2017.

Harlowton

ERIN JONES (GRAF)

TRACK AND FIELD

One of the most decorated athletes in state history, Jones won 22 medals at Class C state meets from 1998-2001 in the 100, 200, 400, 800, 1,600, long jump and on two relay teams, placing her fourth all-time in hardware. In all, Jones won 15 state titles on her own, also good for fourth in the MHSA record book. As a senior in 2001, she won six golds and a silver at the state meet. At Montana State, where she was known as Erin Jones-Graf, she set the school pentathlon record in 2006 with 3,928 points, won two outdoor and two indoor conference titles in the event, and was an All-American in the heptathlon. She also matched the school record in the 100 hurdles. An accomplished artist who also spent time as an assistant track coach at MSU, Jones-Graf was inducted into MSU's Hall of Fame in 2016.

Harrison

JED FIKE

FOOTBALL

Another great small-town all-round athlete, Fike made his mark first at Harrison and then Whitehall in track, basketball and football. Despite breaking his leg in his senior season, he put on a dominating performance—rushing for 194 yards and four TDs—in the Class B all-star game in 2015 before moving on to start his collegiate career at Dickinson State. Fike subsequently transferred to Montana Tech, where he became one of the NAIA's most dominant running backs before experiencing an injury-plagued senior season in 2019. He led the Frontier Conference in rushing for two consecutive seasons, and was fourth in the nation as a junior in rushing yardage.

Havre

MARC MARIANI

FOOTBALL

A winner of 10 letters at Havre High, including four in tennis—winning two Class A doubles titles with best friend Gary Wagner—Mariani excelled most in football, where his 16 TD receptions in 2004 remain the second most in Class A history. Mariani walked on at Montana and after two nondescript years finished with two All-American seasons. His 29 career TD receptions are a school record and 3,018 yards receiving are second best. Mariani starred as a return specialist in the NFL, earning a Pro Bowl nod for his 2010 season with the Tennessee Titans, the team that drafted him. He spent seven years in the NFL, retiring with the Titans in 2016 after spending two seasons with the Chicago Bears. Mariani is now a real estate agent in Nashville, Tennessee.

Hays

ALBERT HAWLEY

FOOTBALL

A standout athlete from the Fort Belknap Assiniboine/Gros Ventre tribe, Hawley played three years (1925-27) collegiately for what is now the Haskell Indian Nations University in Lawrence, Kansas, where played the entire 11-game 1927 season without missing a single minute. He then transferred to Davis & Elkins College, where he was a two-time captain and two-time honorable mention All-American as a varsity center. Hawley later coached at Indian schools in Idaho and Nevada, winning a high school football state title with the Stewart Indian School in Carson City, and he was AAU boxing commissioner in Nevada. He was inducted into the American Indian Athletic Hall of Fame in 1973, the Davis & Elkins Hall of Fame in 1978, the Nevada Athletic Hall of Fame and the Montana Indian Athletic Hall of Fame in 2009. After a stint in the Navy during World War II, Hawley earned a master's degree from Stanford. He died in 1999.

Heart Butte

MIKE CHAVEZ

BASKETBALL

Any conversation about the state's Indian basketball legends must include Chavez, who was an all-stater for four years—two at Heart Butte, two at Browning—and won three state titles, including two for Heart Butte (2000-01). He was chosen *USA Today* Montana Player of the Year three times. Heavily recruited, Chavez chose to play for Montana, where he had an up-and-down career but eventually earned degrees in anthropology and Native American studies in 2007. Chavez was the No. 1 pick of the the Great Falls Explorers of the Continental Basketball Association in 2007 and also played professionally in Mexico. When his hoops career ended, he became an assistant coach at Little Big Horn College in Crow Agency. In 2020, Chavez was the athletic director and boys basketball coach at Northern Cheyenne for the second time.

Helena

PAT DONOVAN

FOOTBALL

A four-time Pro Bowler with the Dallas Cowboys during a nine-year career (1975-83), Donovan was considered one of the best offensive tackles in the NFL—and some argue he's the greatest football player Montana has ever produced. He is one of only five Cowboys players to earn four Pro Bowl invitations. Donovan, a member of the Stanford University Hall of Fame and the school's All-Century team, was an All-American in football and basketball first at Helena Central and then at Helena High, where he also won six gold medals in track. He was the first two-sport All-American at Helena High; one magazine rated him among the top 30 high school basketball players in the country. In track, he was a five-time state champion, three times in the shot put and twice in the discus, and just for dexterity also was a champion on the Bengals' 880 relay team in 1971. Donovan, who left Helena with four school records in track, now lives in Whitefish.

Helmville

THE MANNIX FAMILY

FOOTBALL

The Mannix name is synonymous with ranching and sports in the upper Blackfoot River Valley, and the achievements filter into four arenas at Drummond High School. In 2009 alone, Neil, Jordan and Bryan Mannix all were all-state in football as the Trojans rolled to an unbeaten season and an 8-Man crown. Perhaps the best of the bunch, Neil was the MVP of the Western C basketball tournament the following winter and he continued his success as a sprinter in track, and Joe was an all-conference honoree in hoops. Another Mannix, Erica, was an all-conference volleyball player in 2006. Most recently the stars were Danny Mannix (football) and Ashley (volleyball). Preceding all of them as early as the 1970s were Brent, Rene, Logan and Cole.

Photo: Bryan Mannix, left; Neil Mannix, right

Highwood

REECE GLIKO

BASKETBALL

To this day, Gliko remains the most prolific boys scorer in state history, amassing 2,763 points from 1990-93, more than 300 ahead of Kirk Walker of Darby. His 928 points in 1990-91 also are a state mark and his 825 a year later rank fifth; his 33.1 points per game in '90-91 also has yet to be surpassed. Gliko, who played his final high school season at Belt, spent two years at Rocky Mountain College and another two at MSU Billings, where he was an All-American and briefly owned the Pacific West Conference record for 3-pointers in a season. For MSU Billings, he led NCAA Division II in scoring and in 3-pointers per game in 1996-97. Gliko played professionally overseas before returning to become an assistant coach first with the Yellowjackets and later with MSU-Northern. He has been coaching basketball in Loveland, Colorado, for the past decade.

Hilger

KARI VOSEN

BASKETBALL

A member of a powerhouse basketball team at Winifred in the mid-1990s—seven graduates from 1996-97 played college basketball—Vosen was second-team all-state as a senior center for a high school team that placed five on the first team. She went on to become a top scorer and strong rebounder for Dawson Community College and then Montana Western. She now lives in southwest Montana.

Hingham

SKIP HARDEN

BASKETBALL

A guard with a penchant for rebounding, Harden was among the state's top players from 1967-71, collecting 1,550 points for an 18.0 average over four years for a Hingham team that finished runnerup in Class C in 1970. During his senior season in 1970-71, the 5-foot-11 playmaker earned all-state honors after averaging 25 points and 20 rebounds per game. Harden went on to become a reliable scorer for the College of Great Falls and eventually a businessman in Missoula.

Hinsdale

WAYNE SYNAN

BASKETBALL

Synan led Hinsdale to its greatest moment in sports in 1988, averaging 27 points and 7 rebounds per game to earn MVP honors as the Raiders won their only Class C state basketball championship. He scored 36 points in the triple-overtime championship game win against Geraldine and averaged 22 points his senior season. Synan also was a record holder in the 400 and 800, where he was a state champion in both. He continued his basketball career at Northern Montana College (now MSU-Northern). Synan remained in the area after college.

Hobson

CHARLES MADDOX

FOOTBALL

An elusive wide receiver, Maddox still holds the state record for yards receiving in a game with 282 set in 1987 against Belt. His mark is 32 yards ahead of runner-up James Lee of Gardiner. Maddox also was a high-scoring all-conference basketball player and an accomplished sprinter in track.

Hogeland

JIM WIRT

BASKETBALL

A prolific scorer, Wirt was known to top 40 points for a northeastern Montana high school that struggled to remain open from its inception in 1929 due to lack of students. He compiled more than 1,500 points for his career, which ended in 1968—two years before the school burned and was permanently shuttered. Wirt went on to college at Northern Montana. Wirt remained in the area after college and has competed in the Montana State Senior Golf Tournament.

Hot Springs

TODD RIECH

TRACK AND FIELD

The trophies for 1988 and '89 Class C track and field titles read "Hot Springs" but they might as well read "Todd Riech." The multi-sport star—he was all-state in basketball, where he averaged 27 points per game as a junior and 30.9 as a senior—single-handedly won those state meets, taking 11 gold medals over three seasons. In 1987, he won the 100, 200, 400 and javelin at the Class C meet, a year later as a senior he duplicated the feat, setting a state record in the 400. After turning down football and basketball scholarships, he was a three-time All-American in the javelin at Fresno State, setting an NCAA record in 1994 en route to winning gold. An Olympian, he won the 1996 Olympic Trials with a record throw but finished 17th at the Atlanta Games. In 2000, he finished third at the Olympic Trials. His best international finish was third at the 1995 Pan American Games. Riech became a certified personal trainer and coach, eventually coaching at the U.S. Olympic Training Center in Chula Vista, California, and co-founding a company in southern California called ProSport Physical Therapy & Performance.

Huntley

CLAY TRYAN

RODEO

A native of the Flaxville area and part of a renowned rodeo family now associated with Billings, Tryan learned the ropes growing up in Huntley and has since become one of Montana's most decorated cowboys. He has qualified for the National Finals Rodeo as a team roper (header) 17 times starting in 2001 and owns three world titles, most recently in 2014. Tryan also has two Tour Finale crowns. For his career, he has earned nearly $2.6 million. In 2010, Clay along with brothers Travis and Brady became the first brother trio to qualify for the NFR in team roping in the same year. Tryan was still active in 2020, finishing ninth in the world standings and 12th at the National Finals Rodeo.

Hysham

CASS BAUER (BILODEAU)

BASKETBALL

This small-town girl made it big, rising from the ranks of the Class C game to starring for Montana State and eventually playing in two professional leagues domestically as well as overseas. At MSU, Bauer was a three-time honorable mention All-American, was Big Sky Conference player of the year in 1994 and departed as the school's leading career scorer with more than 1,400 points. In 1993, she led the Bobcats to their first Big Sky crown, beating Montana twice in eight days at Brick Breeden Fieldhouse in front of huge crowds. After college, she played in the ill-fated American Basketball League—winning a championship—and also in the WNBA, where she played in two playoff games and remains the only MSU alum to play in the league. At Hysham, Bauer once scored 56 points in a game. She is enshrined in the MSU Hall of Fame. After receiving a master's degree in healthcare management, Bauer moved to Richland, Washington, where she is a regional director for outreach, development and telemedicine for a hospital.

Ingomar

ROD NEWMAN

BASKETBALL

More than a half-century ago, Newman set a school record that'll never be broken unless the school in Ingomar were to reopen—a dubious prospect given that Ingomar High was only open five years. In 1966, the 5-foot-10 junior guard scored 56 points in a game against Reed Point, a state record then and a mark that remains the ninth-highest in state history for boys, per the MHSA record book. The record would stand for 17 years, until Gary Whiteman of Lodge Grass scored 60. In a family of accomplished athletes, including his high-scoring brother Stan, Newman also was an outstanding high school saddle bronc rider.

Inverness

DARWIN CADY

FOOTBALL

An all-star running back and guard for the football team, Cady—a member of a prolific family of Hi-Line athletes—helped lead the Cardinals to the District 6C football championship in 1974. He also was a consistent scorer for the basketball team, frequently pouring in 20 points or more. Cady was picked for the 1975 East-West Shrine Game in football. He also was a district champion in the javelin and a top competitor in the shot put.

Ismay

JOE MONTANA

FOOTBALL

OK, this one is a bit of a stretch. But the southeast Montana town actually renamed itself "Joe, Montana"after the NFL Hall of Fame quarterback as part of a publicity stunt by a Kansas City radio station in 1993. Montana never visited the little railroad town (pop. 19), but the entire community did get to meet with him in Kansas City. A community building still has a sign that reads "Joe, Montan" (the 'a' dropped off in a windstorm). An athlete actually from Ismay would be a tossup between 1978 Rodeo Hall of Fame inductee Bob Askin, who won major bronc-riding competitions across the country, and his best friend, Paddy Ryan, also a 1978 Hall of Fame inductee.

Jackson

FRED HIRSCHY

RODEO

A steer wrestler and team roper, Hirschy rose to prominence on the Montana Pro Rodeo Circuit in the 1970s and continued to compete into the 1990s as an all-around cowboy. In 1990, he sat atop the Montana PRCA standings in steer wrestling and all-around ahead of legend Dan Mortenson after the summer Cowboy Christmas. That same summer Hirschy was steer wrestling champion at the Buffalo Bill Cody Stampede, and the previous year he was steer wrestling champ at Helena's Last Chance Stampede. A rancher in the picturesque upper Big Hole Valley—Anheuser-Busch once filmed a beer commercial on his property—Hirschy has helped preserve the Big Hole River's struggling Arctic grayling population by relinquishing some of his water rights.

Joliet

MACKENZIE O'DORE

CROSS COUNTRY

In 2010, O'Dore won her third consecutive state cross country championship in record-breaking fashion in Helena, shattering the Class C mark by eight seconds. In the spring, she was nearly as formidable on the track in the 3,200, 1,600 and 800. O'Dore ran for Montana State and Rocky Mountain College, and at Rocky she twice qualified for the NAIA national meet as well as the national outdoor track meet. In the summer of 2019, O'Dore won the prestigious Montana Mile at the Big Sky State Games.

Joplin

JUSTIN MAY

FOOTBALL

Raised on the family wheat farm north of Joplin on the Hi-Line, May had plenty of options in 2017 after three-time all-state careers in football and basketball as well as winning a Class C state title in the long jump in track. A running back/linebacker at Chester-Joplin-Inverness, May opted for football at Montana Tech after receiving offers in all three sports—including interest from Montana State. May started immediately at safety for Montana Tech, and as a freshman in 2017 led the team in tackles before finishing third in '18 and fourth in '19.

Jordan

JERRY KRAMER

FOOTBALL

For the foreseeable future, the most remote county seat in the Lower 48 states gets to stake its claim as the only town in Montana with a native son in the NFL Hall of Fame. Kramer, who spent the first five years of his life in Jordan and then another year in Helena, played football at Idaho before embarking on a legendary 11-year NFL career with the Green Bay Packers. Kramer's famous block in the 1967 "Ice Bowl" provided just enough room for quarterback Bart Starr to sneak into a frozen end zone to beat the Dallas Cowboys and qualify for the first Super Bowl. He was all-pro five times and co-authored the best-selling book *Instant Replay*. Kramer, who was inducted into the NFL Hall of Fame in 2018, now lives in southwest Idaho. He is in the Wisconsin Athletic Hall of Fame and a member of the NFL's 50th anniversary all-time team. A street in his native town is named after a member of the family who platted the Garfield County seat, and one of his sons, Jordan, who also played in the NFL, was named for the town.

Judith Gap

BAILEY SNELLING

BASKETBALL

Snelling was almost unstoppable as a four-year starter for the Harlowton Engineers, leading her team to a 99-7 record and scoring more than 2,000 points. She still holds the state record for career 3-pointers with 295 and ranks 10th all-time in scoring. An all-round athlete, she also was Class C state golf champion in 2010 after finishing fourth as a junior. Snelling played basketball for Carroll College, where she was the team's leading scorer and all-conference her junior and senior years. An Academic All-American, she scored more than 1,000 career points at Carroll. Today Snelling is an elementary school teacher and assistant basketball coach in Harlowton.

Kalispell

ALICE RITZMAN

GOLF

In a 20-year career on the LPGA Tour (1978-98), Ritzman had the distinction of being the highest-ranked player in history without a tour victory. She earned nearly $1.5 million in 401 events and was as close to a victory as three playoff losses, two of them in 1981—to Hall of Fame golfers Kathy Whitworth and Hollis Stacy. The third was in '86 to another future Hall of Famer, Betsy King. When she retired, she ranked 35th on the career LPGA money list and is still 43rd, also the highest for a golfer who never won a tournament. In her first year on the tour, she became the first and only LPGA golfer to record three eagles in one round, at the Colgate European Open in 1979; it remains an LPGA Tour record. In her home state, she won the Montana State Amateur in 1972 and 1973, and attended Eastern Montana College. After retiring from the LPGA Tour, she played on the Legends Tour and worked as an ESPN commentator. Today, Ritzman is a Realtor in Kalispell.

Kevin

KORY FROST

GOLF

A high school basketball all-star and standout running back on the football team for Sunburst in the mid-1970s, Frost made an even bigger name for himself in golf. He was consistently among the top players in the state as a Class C golfer competing against the big schools. Frost, who now lives and competes out of Trabuco Canyon, California, upped his amateur game after college. In August 2019, he made the round of 16 at the U.S. Senior Amateur Golf Tournament in Durham, North Carolina. As of September 2019, he was ranked among the top 100 senior amateur golfers in the nation by Golfweek. His top finish that year was 12th in the Trans-Miss Senior and Mid-Master tournament.

Kinsey

JACK WITCHER

RODEO

A member of a Rodeo Hall of Fame family, Witcher began riding bulls and broncs in high school, and eventually earned second- and third-place finishes in calf roping at the Calgary Stampede in the early 1970s. In 1977, he was calf roping champion on the Montana PRCA Circuit. In the early 1980s, he won world championships in the PRCA Old Timer's Rodeo. The Witcher family was inducted into the Montana Pro Rodeo Hall and Wall of Fame in 2018.

Kirby

JERRY SMALL

RODEO

Few Indian cowboys could rope like the Northern Cheyenne's Small, who won the all-around and steer wrestling crowns at the Montana Pro Rodeo Circuit Finals in 1979 and added another all-around buckle plus a tie-down roping title in 1985. At the Indian National Finals Rodeo, he was an all-around champion five times, dominating in the early 1980s. Small's achievements earned him induction in both the Montana Pro Rodeo Hall of Fame and the Indian National Finals Rodeo Hall of Fame. He died in August 2019 at age 66.

Kremlin

KIM BERG

TRACK AND FIELD

One day after Sidney's Hanna Warfield set the state javelin IAAF record in 2002, Berg shattered it with a toss of 140-3—and that was just the beginning. Berg, also a volleyball and basketball standout at Kremlin-Guilford's North Star High School, was a high school state champion in the javelin and highly competitive in the long jump, high jump and shot put as well. She was even better in college, never losing a javelin competition against Big Sky Conference foes in four years at Montana State. She won four consecutive conference championships despite having three ACL surgeries in her career. In 2007, Berg qualified for the NCAA Outdoor Track & Field Championships and was ranked 23rd nationally. She was the Big Sky's Field Event Athlete of the Year in 2008.

Lambert

JEREMY LAKE

BASKETBALL

Back when Lambert was flying solo in high school sports, the Lions made a run at the 1990 state championship (losing to Box Elder) behind the formidable tag-team of Rusty Vaira and Lake, who averaged more than 20 points per game over four years. Lake, an all-conference tight end in football and outstanding hurdler and high jumper as well, averaged 26 points, 9 rebounds and 6 assists in his senior year. At Montana, he led the team in scoring in 1992-93 and left as the leading 3-point scorer in Big Sky Conference history. Lake entered his junior season as the nation's top returning free-throw shooter and set school records for career and single-season free-throw percentage. A pre-med student, Lake also was an academic All-American who attended medical school at the University of Washington and now is a gastroenterologist in Hillsboro, Oregon.

Lame Deer

KENNY BIG BACK

FOOTBALL/BASKETBALL

Noted for his flair on the football field and basketball court, Big Back was an all-stater in both sports for the Colstrip Colts. After high school, he moved on to Rocky Mountain College, where he was first-team all-conference and honorable mention All-American in basketball in 1996. Big Back was inducted into the Montana Indian Athletic Hall of Fame in 2014. Today, Big Back is a heavy equipment operator for Westmoreland Coal Co. out of Colstrip and resides in Lame Deer with his family.

Laurel

PATRICK CASEY

TRACK AND FIELD

A world-class distance runner, Casey's dream of an Olympic berth in 2016 was shut down by chronic plantar fasciitis. Nevertheless, he remains one of the state's most decorated 1,500-meter runners ever, finishing runner-up in the USA Championships in 2014 and then fourth in 2018 after recovering from foot surgery. He still holds the Montana State school record for the indoor mile (3:54.59) and 800, and he was a three-time All-American for the Bobcats before transferring to Oklahoma. At Laurel, Casey was an All-American and a six-time state champion, sweeping cross country and the 800, 1,600 and 3,200 meters his senior year. He is the first runner to break four minutes in the mile on Montana soil and is a multi-winner of the Montana Mile.

Laurin

TIFF MYERS

BASEBALL

Myers was a three-sport star who played football and basketball for both Twin Bridges and Ennis, and American Legion baseball for the Dillon Cubs in the early 2000s. In football, he was an all-conference center, linebacker and fullback for Twin Bridges. Myers played baseball collegiately at Lewis-Clark State. After college, he played for the Helena Titans in the ill-fated Rocky Mountain Football League.

Lavina

KEITH MASON

TRACK AND FIELD

A great all-round athlete, Mason held records in the high jump and hurdles when he was at Lavina but saved his best work for college. After starting at the University of Montana, he transferred to Rocky Mountain College, where he competed in four sports in the early 1950s. Mason was captain of the football team, frequently scored 20 points in basketball, lettered in baseball and was one of the most dominant collegiate track athletes in the state. He scored 24.7 points in a dual meet against Eastern Montana College and had 20.5 in a meet at Bozeman as a senior in 1953. Immediately out of college, Mason took a job as head basketball and track coach at Harlowton before resigning to enter dentistry school. He was inducted into Rocky's Hall of Fame in 1994.

Lewistown

JIM OTTEN

BASEBALL

By the time he reached high school and was playing American Legion baseball Otten was living in Kalispell and earning attention from college coaches. As a pitcher, he was 16-3 and 12-1 in back-to-back years leading Mesa (Ariz.) Community College to national championships before moving on to Arizona State. Otten later appeared in 64 Major League Baseball games, first for the Chicago White Sox and then for the St. Louis Cardinals. He had one big-league victory. Otten was inducted in the Mesa CC Hall of Fame in 2006. After his nine-year Major League career, he became a project manager for a cable TV engineering company and eventually began his own company in the Phoenix suburb of Mesa.

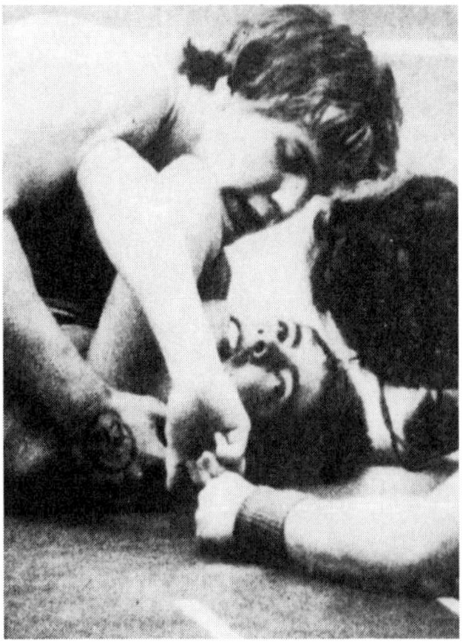

Libby

TERRY MAKI

WRESTLING/FOOTBALL

A three-time state wrestling champion, Maki went 86-1 in his career for the Loggers and probably would've been unbeaten had he not fractured an elbow. He also was an all-state football player and signed a letter of intent with Montana State initially after graduation in 1982. Maki later opted to attend the Air Force Academy on a wrestling scholarship and as a football walk-on. In football, he was a first-team all-conference linebacker as a junior and a Kodak All-American as a senior. He still holds the Air Force school record for tackles in a career (475), season (195) and game (30). After his 30-tackle game in an upset of Notre Dame, in which he also blocked a field goal that was returned for a TD, he was national Defensive Player of the Week. Maki also managed to find time to wrestle for the Falcons, earning the Western Athletic Conference's Outstanding Wrestler award as a sophomore. After his competitive career ended, he went into coaching in the Bitterroot.

Lima

ALISON SCOTT

BASKETBALL

Never heard of Scott? Neither has the MHSA record book even though she was the third girl ever to score more than 2,000 points in a career (2,047). A 5-foot-6 guard, Scott led the Bears to their first state tournament appearance as a senior in 1994. She averaged 22 points per game and was chosen to the *USA Today* honorable mention All-America team. Scott actually averaged more points as a sophomore (26) and junior (30). She was an all-purpose athlete on the Lima track team, competing in the sprints, high jump, long jump and triple jump. Scott eventually walked on to the Western Montana College basketball team. She now lives in Dillon and her son, Troy Scott, also played at UMW.

Lincoln

DOUG SWINGLEY

MUSHER

In Alaska, "Swingley" is two four-letter words, thanks to the Great Falls native and former Simms resident's habit of tormenting Alaskans after earning a landmark victory in the Iditarod Trail Sled Dog Race in 1995—the first by a musher from the Lower 48 states. Swingley, nicknamed "The Cowboy" by Alaskans, went on to win three more Iditarods, leaving him one shy of all-time record holder Rick Swenson, and he remains the only non-Alaskan from the U.S. to win that state's Super Bowl. Along the way, Swingley was Rookie of the Year in 1992, set the Iditarod speed record in 1995 and again in 2000, and was the event's oldest winner ever when he reached the burled arch in Nome first in 1999. He's also won Montana's Race to the Sky.

Livingston

LARRY QUESTAD

TRACK AND FIELD

For a brief time in the early 1960s, Questad was considered the fastest human in the world and for nearly a decade was routinely described as the "world's fastest white man." He was NCAA 100-yard dash champion at Stanford in 1963 in 9.3, won the 100 and 200 at the World Games in Finland, and was one-tenth of a second behind Bob Hayes in qualifying for the 1964 Olympics. In 1968, Questad was the third 200 sprinter on the U.S. Olympic Team in Mexico City with John Carlos and Tommie Smith, who became infamous for raising their black-gloved fists on the medal stand in protest of social injustice. Questad ran a 9.6 in the 100 and 21.0 in the 220 for Park High School in Livingston in 1961 before Montana converted to meters, both state records. He lived for many years and owned a business in Boise, Idaho, where he passed away in October 2020.

Lockwood

DAN MORTENSEN

RODEO

Among Montana's prolific list of rodeo stars, none surpass Mortensen, who was the 1997 world all-around champion and also won six saddle bronc championships. He participated in 16 National Finals Rodeos, missing only one in his career (2004) thanks to a broken ankle; he was nevertheless leading the world standings at the time. In 2003, his sixth time winning a saddle bronc title, he became the first PRCA roughstock cowboy to earn $2 million; he ultimately finished with $2.55 million. In 1994, Mortensen won the NFR average crown and in 2002 he won a bronze medal at the Winter Olympics. He was inducted into the Pro Rodeo Hall of Fame in 2009, a year after his 2008 retirement, and a statue outside the MetraPark Arena in Billings reflects his stature in the sport. *Sports Illustrated* rated him the No. 2 athlete of all time for Montana. Mortensen, who competed collegiately at Northwest College in Powell, Wyoming, and won a national saddle bronc title at Montana State, later coached rodeo at Northwest. He is enshrined in MSU's Athletic Hall of Fame.

Lodge Grass

ELVIS OLD BULL

BASKETBALL

Nicknamed "Montana's Magic," Old Bull was one of those rare superstars whose skills were so mythical they transcended the game. From 1988-90, he led Lodge Grass to three consecutive Class B state titles, earning tournament MVP all three years. Over four seasons, Old Bull scored more than 1,900 points, set 16 school records, averaged nearly 20 points per game and once had 22 assists in a single game. In 1989, he scored nine points in 36 seconds to rally Lodge Grass past Cut Bank for the Class B state title. A registered Crow, Old Bull never played in college but he is in the Montana Indian Athletic Hall of Fame and was the only high school athlete listed among *Sports Illustrated*'s top 50 Montanans of all time in 1999. He died in a car accident in 2014.

Lodgepole

BRAD AND JUSTIN WALSH

WRESTLING

Raised on a ranch on the Fort Belknap Indian Reservation between Zortman and Lodgepole, the Walsh boys were part of a heady Malta High wrestling legacy in the late 1980s and early 1990s. Brad was the slightly more accomplished of the two, placing four times at state and winning championships in 1991 and '92—wrestling all four years at 152 pounds. He concluded his illustrious career on the mat with 52 consecutive victories. Brad also was all-conference in football. Older brother Justin was the 145-pound state champ for Malta in 1989, was a four-time state qualifier as well and finished second at the AAU Grand Nationals in 1989. He wrestled three years at what was then Northern Montana College and was nationally ranked as a freshman and sophomore. Justin later was an assistant coach at Billings West.

Lolo

KORY MYTTY

RODEO

Now the University of Montana's rodeo coach, Mytty was a high-level team-roping heeler on the Professional Rodeo Cowboys Association (PRCA) circuit for more than 15 years. He qualified for the College National Finals with Blue Mountain (Ore.) Community College in 1988 and '89. In 1994, Mytty fulfilled a dream by reaching the NFR and he also made the Dodge National Circuit Finals 11 times. Starting that same year, he has consistently been atop the Montana Pro Rodeo Circuit Finals team-roping standings, frequently with header Shane Schwenke of Zortman.

Loring

LANCE WASSON

BASKETBALL

Raised on a farm outside of Loring, Wasson was an all-state football and basketball for Malta in the late 1980s, twice leading the Mustangs to the state hoops tournament and setting school records in the process. He averaged 18 points per game as a senior and went on to play at Northern Montana College, where his father, Alan, played. With the Lights, Wasson raised his game. He started all four years and in 1993 set the school scoring record with 41 points against Western Montana College, a mark that hasn't been broken. In the same game, he shattered the school record with 12 3-point baskets, which also still stands. Wasson ranks 10th on the MSU-Northern career scoring list with 1,253 points from 1989-93 and owns the career and single-season records for 3-pointers with 259 and 104.

Lustre

ROB AND JASON BAKER

BASKETBALL

Raised on the family farm just outside of Lustre, the high-scoring brothers were responsible for some of Lustre Christian's headier basketball days, with Rob compiling 2,023 points and averaging 22.5 points per game from 1985-89. A year younger, Jason was no slouch, either, scoring 1,156 career points for an average of 16.7 per game. Jason was at his best as a senior, when he put up 23 points and 10 rebounds per contest. Rob etched his name in the MHSA record books with a 60-point outing in 1988, tying him for what remains the sixth best single-game performance in state history. Both brothers went on to play for Dawson Community College.

Madoc

JOHN MORRISON

BASKETBALL

Though he might be best known for his offspring, Morrison was nonetheless a three-sport standout athlete who grew up on a farm outside Madoc. He learned to play basketball on a rim attached to his barn and played in a gym with 9-foot ceilings. After averaging 16 points and 13 rebounds as a senior in high school, he played for Northern Montana College and then professionally for two years in The Netherlands and Austria in the '70s before moving into a coaching career that took him back to Northern Montana and to Dawson Community College in Glendive. Along the way he met another talented athlete, Wanda Hames of Peerless, and married her. While Morrison was coaching in Glendive, the couple had a son they named Adam. Soon after, they moved to South Dakota and Wyoming, and finally Morrison retired from coaching, moving the family to Spokane, Washington, where their 8-year-old son became a ballboy for Gonzaga. Adam Morrison would go on to become perhaps Gonzaga's greatest player ever and one of the top college basketball stars from 2003-06, averaging 28.1 points per game his final season with the Zags.

Malta

GRETA KOSS (BUEHLER)

BASKETBALL

In a community renowned for its girls basketball stars, Koss stands out for where she took her career after her time with the M-ettes. She was a cog in the Malta pipeline to the Lady Griz, leading the team to four Big Sky titles from 1994-97, earning two first-team all-Big Sky selections and nabbing conference MVP her junior season. After college, Koss was an original member of the WNBA in 1997, playing 13 games for the Utah Starzz. When Koss was enshrined in the Grizzly Sports Hall of Fame in 2016, she ranked fifth in school history in rebounds and 19th in scoring. Her 20 rebounds against MSU in 1997 set a school single-game record. Koss, now works as office director for the Montana High School Association in Helena, coached the Billings West girls basketball team for five years.

Manhattan

CALEB NETH

TRACK AND FIELD

From 2013-16, Neth was a one-man show for the Tigers in the Class B state meet, racking up 14 state titles—one shy of the record held by Glasgow's Roy Robinson. Neth, who was a jumper, hurdler and sprinter, ranks third all-time with 18 medals at state meets. He won three consecutive long jump titles and two straight in the 400. He now competes in six events at Montana State, where in 2018 he was fourth in the indoor heptathlon in the Big Sky Conference with the eighth-best mark in school history. Neth wasn't bad in football, either, earning all-state honors as a receiver, defensive back and kick returner for Manhattan in 2015. Oh, and he won the Wheat Montana Junior Golf Tour in 2010.

Marysville

FRANK JAMES "BROWNIE" BURKE

BASEBALL

At 4-foot-7 as an adult, Burke wasn't much of an athlete. But he nevertheless was the first native Montanan to make it onto a Major League Baseball field, albeit as a mascot. In 1909, after spending four years as a Senate page in Helena, Burke was working at the Mammoth Hot Springs Hotel as a bellhop when he met Cincinnati Reds president August "Garry" Herrmann, who offered him the team's mascot job after getting permission from his mother. He wore a uniform, served as batboy and even occasionally warmed up a Reds pitcher. It was also Burke's job to tell players they were released and, according to *Montana Baseball History*, he reportedly even spied on players after hours for Herrmann. Another historical footnote: Burke reputedly was the shortest man to serve in the U.S. Army in World War I. He reportedly died either of tuberculosis or pneumonia in Bakersfield, California, in 1931 and is buried in Helena's Resurrection Cemetery.

Medicine Lake

TERRY SCHLABS

TRACK AND FIELD

A basketball and football standout, Schlabs was exceptional on the track and in the field, where he set state records in the triple jump, discus and 110 hurdles while leading Medicine Lake to the 1969 Class C track crown—scoring all 26 of his team's points. At the Eastern C divisional that year, he scored 30 points—five firsts—and set three meet records. Nicknamed "Big Daddy," he was all-conference for three years in football and two years in basketball. Schlabs earned a track scholarship at Montana State and then Eastern Montana College, where as a decathlete he finished sixth nationally in 1973. He was inducted into the MHSA Athletes' Hall of Fame in 2007. Schlabs lives in Spirit Lake, Idaho, where he is a real estate broker specializing in lakefront property and acreage.

Melrose

BENNY REYNOLDS

RODEO

An all-around cowboy, Reynolds was among the top 10 competitors at the National Finals Rodeo in all 11 of his appearances in bareback riding, steer wrestling and bull riding. He was the 1960 NFR Average Bareback Champion, the 1961 World All-Around Champion, and the Reserve All-Around Champion in 1964. A graduate of Beaverhead High in Dillon, Reynolds is one of two Montanans to ever win the Linderman Award, given to the contestant earning the most money in a combination of three or more roughstock and timed events. Reynolds was Rodeo Cowboys Association rookie of the year in 1958 and won seven all-around titles at the National Old-Timers Rodeo Association finals. In 1958, Reynolds appeared on a TV quiz show *Name That Tune*, where he was famous for his one-word "Yup" answers. He was inducted into the ProRodeo Hall of Fame in 1993. Reynolds died in 2014 while loading hay at his Twin Bridges ranch.

Melstone

BRODY GREBE

BASKETBALL

It's difficult to know which sport to associate Grebe with, because he was equally accomplished in four in high school—football, basketball, track and rodeo. He was quarterback for Class B Roundup in 2018, leading the team to a 10-1 record as a senior while scoring 31 touchdowns. In basketball, Grebe averaged 28 points, 10 rebounds and five assists for Melstone and finished with more than 2,500 career points, scoring 50 in a game in February 2019 and setting a school record with 10 3-pointers. Then came gold medals in the shot put, long jump and triple jump in track. And he was one of the state's top high school tie-down and team ropers. After high school Grebe, a 4.0 student, attended a prep school on the East Coast and was weighing offers from several Ivy League schools before committing to Montana State for football.

Miles City

RUSS SWEET

TRACK AND FIELD

A football, basketball and track standout at Montana from 1924-26, Sweet placed second in 100- and 200-yard dashes at the 1925 NCAA championships shortly after setting school records (9.7 and 21.4) in both events at the Pacific Coast Conference meet. In 1924, he was second in the nation in scoring in football with 75 points and caught the game-winning touchdown pass from Montana legend and Hall of Famer William "Wild Bill" Kelly and kicked the extra point in a 7-3 win for the West in the East-West Shrine game. Sweet left school early to compete for the Olympic Club in San Francisco in track and football. His 9.4 in the 100 in 1928 would've been a world record had it not been deemed wind-aided. Sweet led Miles City to the 1922 state football championship and set several state and West Coast records in the sprints. He was inducted into the Grizzly Sports Hall of Fame in 1993. Sweet died in 1944.

Missoula

DAVE JOHNSON

TRACK AND FIELD

Remember Dan and Dave, the subjects of the famous Reebok commercials leading up to the 1992 Barcelona Olympics? That was Dave Johnson, an Olympic decathlete who, along with Dan O'Brien, was considered one of the two greatest athletes in the world at the time. Johnson was born in Missoula and attended Sentinel High School before moving to Corvallis, Oregon, for his final year. He played football at Azusa Pacific for two years before starting his decathlon career. After setting the American decathlon record with 8,549 points in 1988, Johnson made the Olympic team and finished ninth. Four years later, he won the bronze medal after what remains one of the most famous sports advertising campaigns in history. Johnson now works with the Fellowship of Christian Athletes in Oregon.

Photo: Dave Johnson, left

Moccasin

JOE AND NED ASHCRAFT

BASEBALL

Both three-sport standouts, the two were especially gifted as infielders in baseball in the late 1960s and early '70s. Joe, two years older, immediately started collegiately as a second baseman and shortstop at Northern Montana, and he was followed soon after by Ned, who transferred from Eastern Montana. Ned was the better all-round athlete, also playing end on the football team for the Lights after a distinguished high school career. At Moccasin and Stanford, Ned and Joe also routinely pumped in 20 points or more on the basketball court; both were second-team all-district picks in 1965, when Joe was a senior and Ned a sophomore. Joe now lives in Ketchikan, Alaska, where he owns a telecommunications company, and Ned is in Missoula, where he owns an electrical contractor business.

Molt

HANK HOLLENBECK

RODEO

Hollenbeck is a two-time Montana PRCA Pro Rodeo Circuit all-around champion and owns a year-end title in tie-down roping. He won the all-around title in 2014, 2015 and 2017. In the summer of 2019, he won the tie-down roping en route to being the top all-around cowboy at the Little Big Horn Stampede Rodeo in Hardin and also was top all-around cowboy at the PRCA Thermopolis rodeo. At Rapelje High, Hollenbeck—known then as "Henry"—was a football and basketball standout. In 2002, he was the top scorer in District 5C basketball at 22.1 points per game while earning second-team Class C all-state honors. In football, he was first-team all-conference as a tight end and kicker in the 6-Man South and second-team defensive lineman.

Montana City

SABRINA MONRO

CROSS COUNTRY

A product of Jefferson High in Boulder, Monro achieved the best performance ever by a University of Montana runner at the NCAA Division I cross country championships by finishing second in 2000, seven seconds behind the winner. That was shortly after she won her second Big Sky Conference title. Monro transferred for her senior season to Washington, where she opened the 2001 season with four victories, set two course records and appeared in *Sports Illustrated*'s Faces In The Crowd before suffering a stress fracture. In her only indoor competition that winter, Monro set a school record in the 3,000. Monro was Class B state champion in cross country, the 1,600 and the 3,200, winning the latter two events as a junior and a senior and setting a state mark in the 1,600. In 2010, Monro was hired to coach girls cross country at Capital High in Helena.

Moore

PAUL BARTA

TRACK AND FIELD

A gifted playmaker and all-district player for Moore High, Barta went on to excel in basketball and track at Rocky Mountain College in the mid-1970s. He was the Frontier Conference six-mile champion as a senior in 1978 and finished 34th in the NAIA marathon a month later in only his second 26.2-mile run. Barta made an even bigger name for himself as a high school coach. leading the Columbus boys team for 29 years and guiding the Cougars to Class B runner-up finishes five times. He then took on the girls program as well, nabbing another second-place finish at state in 2001. Barta most recently was coach of the boys basketball program at Laurel until stepping down after the 2019-20 season. He was inducted into Rocky Mountain College's Hall of Fame in 2016.

Muddy Creek

CLIFFORD FOOTE

TRACK AND FIELD

Though Muddy Creek isn't technically a Montana town, it's certainly a community to the Northern Cheyenne—and no family reflects its athletic prowess more than the Footes, especially Clifford. Four years after his cousin Raymond Harris won the last of three state mile championships for Colstrip in 1962, and then his brother Richard went back-to-back in '63 and '64, Clifford set the interscholastic record in '66 with a mark of 4:28.2 running for St. Labre. By then, he already owned the state two-mile record. A year later, he bested his time by four seconds in winning the mile at the Montana USATF championships. Foote also was a state Class B cross country champion, owned the Southern C divisional record in the 880, and also competed in the 220 and 440 sprints. He set four cross country records and set the Mon-Dak Conference record at Dawson Community College in addition to winning the All-Indian Championship Decathlon in 1968. Foote died in 2011.

Musselshell

FRANCIS TURLEY

BOXING

A native of Billings who attended Roundup High School to play football and box, Turley grew up near Musselshell in the Bull Mountains. His claim to fame: During a Golden Gloves bout in 1958, he sent an up-and-coming 16-year-old superstar named Cassius Clay (later Muhammad Ali) to the canvas in the second round. In his autobiography *The Greatest*, Ali said, "The hardest I was ever hit was by a Montana cowboy." Turley finished 57-6 as an amateur boxer. As a football player at Roundup High, he was chosen to play in the East-West Shrine Game as a senior. Turley returned to the Bull Mountains after attending Montana State but eventually moved to Texas, where he died in 2016.

Nashua

JON KING

CROSS COUNTRY

King's running acumen stood out early—his time of 16:24.0 in the state's first cross country championship over three miles as a sophomore in 1976 stood for four years at the Class C level and remains the fifth best time. King, who finished second at the state cross country meet in 1977, was one of Montana's more successful competitors in the one- and two-mile events as well.

Nevada City

CONNOR MOORE

BASKETBALL

Moore was a two-time all-conference basketball player who averaged 20 points per game as a senior at Ennis while growing up between the historic mining communities of Nevada City and Virginia City, as well as Alder. He also played football, golfed and was academic all-state for the Mustangs, and was an all-state baseball player for the Gallatin Valley Outlaws in 2009. After playing for the Montana AAU baseball team based out of Three Forks, he walked on to the basketball team at Idaho State from 2010-12. He played once in his first year, against Montana State, and twice as a sophomore.

Noxon

DAN BEAUDIN

FOOTBALL

Nicknamed "Chief," Beaudin was a 6-foot-5 quarterback for Noxon's 8-Man football team, but switched to tight end and defensive end when he arrived at Montana. An all-round athlete who earned all-state honors in leading Noxon to the Class C basketball tournament in 2004, he was a standout thrower in track and field, finishing second in the Big Sky championships for UM in the discus. He was even recruited to join the injury-plagued Griz basketball team midseason in 2008. After back-to-back honorable mention all-conference honors, Beaudin eventually earned a brief tryout with the Miami Dolphins of the NFL. He is now a teacher in Missoula.

Oilmont

DON SAUBY

BASKETBALL

Sauby was a standout in both basketball and football in the late 1950s for Oilmont, an ill-fated school on the southern tip of the Sunburst Oil Field on the Hi-Line. Sauby routinely scored 20-plus points in games and found the end zone for the Trojans' 6-Man football team. Oilmont, which had its finest basketball teams during Sauby's era, closed its doors in 1984. Sauby lives in Cut Bank and was a manager for a concrete company.

Opheim

GWEN DIGHANS

BASKETBALL

Dighans did it all for the Vikings, but saved her best for basketball, where she led her team to three consecutive Class C state championships. She was tournament MVP in leading Opheim to the 1983 and '84 titles. A 6-foot-2 center, she averaged 20 points and nearly 10 rebounds per game in the '83 tournament and earned *USA Today* honorable mention All-America honors. Dighans, who was first-team all-state three times in basketball, also was a standout in the discus and shot put in track and field. She continued her basketball career collegiately at Idaho and started as a sophomore but eventually transferred to Northern Montana College (now MSU-Northern), where she was one of the team's top scorers her final two seasons.

Opportunity

ROGER ROUSE

BOXING

The son of a mining foreman, Rouse started boxing as a 9-year-old in the back of the Wonder Bar in nearby Anaconda. An excellent basketball player and all-state fullback, he led Anaconda to the Class A state football title in 1951. He started college as a football player at Montana, but a knee injury halted his football career and he accepted a boxing scholarship to Idaho State, where he twice was an NCAA 165-pound champion. Rouse was a national Golden Gloves champion in 1954 and boxed in the 1956 Olympics in Melbourne, losing in the quarterfinals. As a professional, he was the No. 1 light heavyweight contender in 1965 and fought three times for a world title, losing all three. He had a record of 39-23-4 as a pro from 1958-72. Rouse, who was featured in a lengthy 1967 story in *Sports Illustrated*, is enshrined in Idaho State's Hall of Fame. He died in 1999.

Oswego

CHRIS BAUER

FOOTBALL

A three-sport star at Frazer, Bauer was best known for his play on the football field, where he was an all-state tight end in the late 1980s. As a senior, he played in the East-West all-star game. Bauer also was a handful on the basketball court for the Cubs, frequently tossing in 30 points in 3C action and earning second-team all-conference honors.

Outlook

ROBIN SELVIG

BASKETBALL

As a Hall of Fame women's basketball coach, Selvig needs no introduction to Montana Griz faithful. When he concluded his 38-year coaching career in 2016, his 865 victories ranked eighth all-time among college women coaches. Before that, he was a standout guard for the Griz, earning all-Big Sky honors. At Outlook, he had scoring outputs of 48 and 39 in the 1970 Class C state tournament, and still ranks second all-time with 833 points in a single season (1969-70). He also was one of two members of the 1970 state championship track team. Selvig was inducted into the Grizzly Sports Hall of Fame in 2001 and in 2008 became the first non-Indian inducted into the Montana Indian Athletics Hall of Fame for the opportunities he gave to Native players. He is retired and living in Missoula.

Ovando

COLLEEN MCNALLY

BASKETBALL

An all-round athlete at Seeley-Swan, McNally was a four-year starter and two-time all-stater in basketball as a guard, including *USA Today* All-America recognition as a senior in 1987. She also was a three-time letter winner on the track team, where she was a jumper and threw the javelin. McNally went on to become one of the few Class C players for powerhouse teams with the Lady Griz, earning significant playing time before blowing out her right knee in 1989 and her left knee in 1990. McNally eventually became an assistant coach with Montana. A fifth-generation Montanan, she now lives on a conservation-oriented working ranch outside of Ovando and owns the Stray Bullet Café in town.

Park City

BRYAN SEVERIN

BASKETBALL

Easily the most prolific scorer in school history, Severin popped in 56 points in a game for the Panthers in 1991, a mark that ties him for ninth best all-time in Montana history. His career scoring average of 22.76 from 1989-91 ranks him fifth, and his 21 baskets in a single game tie him for ninth in state history. Severin averaged more than 30 points per game as a senior, when he was second-team Class C all-state. He also was an all-star quarterback in football, throwing two TD passes in the 1991 Treasure State Game to lift the Blue past the Red 18-14. Nevertheless, Severin first went to college on a track scholarship, finishing fourth in the javelin at the national junior college meet for the College of Southern Idaho as a freshman in 1992. After a stint in the Navy, he signed five years later to play basketball for Rocky Mountain College, where he was an impact player in his first season.

Peerless

JON AND JOE PUCKETT

BASKETBALL

Back in the 1970s, when District 1C was the most dominant in the state, the twin Puckett brothers were sharp-shooting guards who led their now-defunct school to the Class C state championship game in 1979 against Flaxville, another school no longer open. After topping Flaxville three times during the season, the Panthers fell 66-50. The Pucketts both made the all-tournament team. Joe was first-team all-state in 1978 but Jon was the MVP of the tournament despite the third-place finish. As seniors the following year, they led their team to second in Class C to Flaxville. The Pucketts continued their careers in college—Jon at Montana Tech and Joe at Carroll, before Joe transferred to Tech to rejoin his brother under coach Kelvin Sampson. Joe Puckett, who now works at the Pentagon, went on to write a book about Class C basketball called *The Dream*.

Philipsburg

CARLA BEATTIE

BASKETBALL

When she left Granite High in 1990, Beattie was Montana's all-time leading scorer with 2,005 points, a mark that stood for a decade. Her name still dots the MHSA record book, where she's now third in career scoring, second for a season (882 points) and fourth in points per game (25.8). Beattie's 33.9 points per game in 1990 are second only to Kayla Lambert's 42.2, and her 565 made free throws for a career rank No. 1. A volleyball and javelin standout as well, she played basketball for Montana, where she left in 1996 as one of the program's best 3-point shooters ever and the school's NCAA Woman of the Year. After college, she married Seth Cunneen and became a military wife before the family moved to Midland, Texas, where he works in oil and gas exploration. Beattie taught school, eventually became athletic director and girls basketball coach at Midland Classic Academy, and won four state championships before resigning her coaching position in July 2020 to spend more time watching her niece, Leia Beattie, play at Montana State.

Pinesdale

LANCE ALLRED

BASKETBALL

Born and raised in a fundamentalist polygamist Mormon community, Allred has the distinction of being the first legally deaf player in the NBA and the first Mexican-American. Disillusioned with the Pinesdale community, his family left for Salt Lake City when he was 7. A 7-footer, Allred was Utah's Gatorade Player of the Year in 1999 and ranked the best center in the West. He played collegiately for two years at Utah before transferring to Weber State. From 2005-14, Allred played for 15 professional teams, many of them overseas but also the Idaho Stampede sandwiched around a brief but history-making tenure with the Cleveland Cavaliers in 2008. He was released by the Cavs in 2008 after two 10-day stints. In 2009, he wrote his autobiography, entitled *Longshot: The Adventures of a Deaf Fundamentalist Mormon Kid and His Journey to the NBA*, and he currently is an international motivational speaker.

Plains

CASEY JERMYN

CROSS COUNTRY

In a community that produced all-time leading Carroll College basketball scorer Bill Pilgeram, Jermyn is nevertheless in rarified air. He is one of six runners to win three state cross country championships, from 1997-99. He still ranks second and third on the all-time Class B state list with times of 14:55.0 and 15:05.0; he also won three track titles. After high school, Jermyn went on to run for Montana State, where he won the 2002 Big Sky crown. He still ranks third all-time at MSU in the 5,000 meters and seventh in the 3,000, both indoors. Jermyn coaches a state cross country dynasty today at Bozeman High and owns Bozeman Running Co.

Plentywood

TRAVIS WALKER

FOOTBALL

A three-sport athlete first at Fort Benton and then for three years with the Wildcats, Walker was all-state for four years in football (1992-95) and continued his career at Montana, where he was a four-year starter at wide receiver. He was a three-time Class B champion in the long jump and was all-state in basketball while averaging 28 points and 10 rebounds per game in 1994 and scoring 55 points in a tournament game a year later. When his basketball career was over, he ranked fourth all-time in the state in scoring for boys with 2,354 points. Walker played receiver as a freshman and sophomore then moved to quarterback for his junior and senior years, scoring 48 touchdowns. On defense, he had 21 interceptions in his high school career. When he finished collegiately at UM, he was the school's seventh all-time leading pass receiver. Walker was inducted into the MHSA Athletes' Hall of Fame in 2018. He is now the boys and girls basketball coach at Missoula Loyola.

Plevna

VEDIE HIMSL

BASEBALL

The "Pride of Plevna," Himsl spent 60 years in baseball as a player, coach and finally scouting director with the Chicago Cubs. Born in 1917 in Plevna, he was an all-state basketball and football player, earning letters for four years in each sport and leading the Cossacks to two state hoops crowns. At St. John's (Minn.) University, he earned 10 letters, was all-conference in three sports, and once struck out 20 batters in a game, still a school record. Himsl never made it beyond Class AAA in pro baseball, winning 72 games in the minors. With the Cubs, he was part of owner Philip K. Wrigley's ill-fated "College of Coaches" in 1961, in which the team did away with a manager and instead rotated coaches—and Himsl was the first. His claim to fame as scouting director was discovering future Cubs Hall of Famer Ernie Banks. Himsl died in 2004.

Polson

MELINDA OWEN (WITHROW)

TRACK AND FIELD

A pole vaulter, Owen arrived on the scene by winning the 2003 Class A state championship and setting school records in the pole vault and javelin. A three-sport standout, Owen continued her successful run at Idaho, where she won six indoor and outdoor Western Athletic Conference titles, including three consecutive indoor pole vault golds. Owen finished fifth at the NCAA indoor meet in 2007 and was ranked No. 1 entering the 2008 outdoor meet before suffering an injury. She also competed at the U.S. Olympic Trials three times. Owen, who went on to coach at Montana before returning to Polson as a coach and special education instructor, was inducted into Idaho's Hall of Fame in 2018.

Pompeys Pillar

RANDY SIAN

FOOTBALL

At Huntley Project, Sian was a first-team all-conference guard on defense and center on offense in 1980. He made a name for himself at Rocky Mountain College, where he was a starter beginning with the fourth game of his freshman season in 1981 and earned all-Frontier Conference honors as a sophomore. A smallish noseguard, Sian was a one-man wrecking crew in the middle of the line for Battlin' Bears, racking up 23 tackles—13 for loss—and forcing five fumbles (he recovered four) in a game against Jamestown his junior year. He was Rocky's top tackler that year and as a senior in 1984, when he was the Frontier's MVP on defense. Sian was inducted into Rocky's Hall of Fame in 2001. He owns a farm in Ballantine.

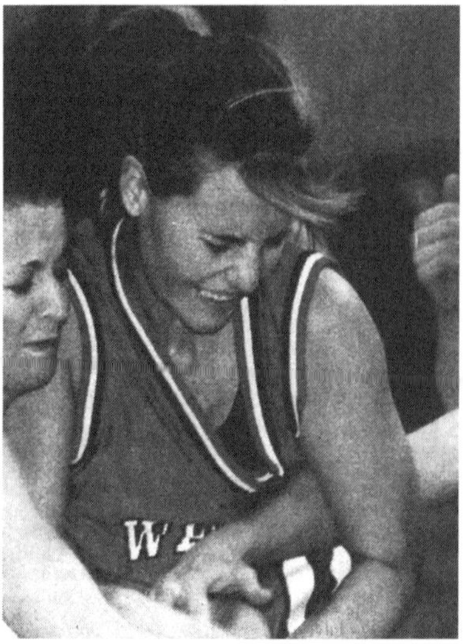

Pony

BOBBI SUHR (KONEN)

BASKETBALL

A multi-sport high school standout down the road at Harrison, Suhr was one of the state's top high school basketball players in the late 1990s, earning first-team Class C all-state honors. She also set a state record in the discus in 1999 while excelling in the shot put and javelin. Before that, Suhr was a sharpshooter with a rifle, earning a berth along with her sister, Jari, at the National Junior Olympic Shooting Championships. Suhr took basketball to another level at Western Montana College, where she was Frontier Conference MVP three times, twice was chosen Kodak first-team All-American, was featured in *Sports Illustrated*'s Faces in the Crowd and remains the Bulldogs' career leading scorer as well as one of the top rebounders. Suhr, who owned the single-season scoring record until Brianna King topped it during the 2018-19 season, was inducted into the Bulldog Hall of Fame in 2015. Today she is a paraprofessional at Dillon Middle School and is an assistant coach with the Dillon girls basketball team.

Poplar

MIKE GRANBOIS

BASKETBALL

With a nod to Scott McGowan—the first Montanan to run a sub-four-minute mile, in 2005—the all-round standout is Granbois, a four-sport star who averaged more than 25 points per game and led the state in scoring in basketball in his senior year in 1950-51, when the Indians won the Class C state title behind his 23 points. A native of Medicine Lake, Granbois also starred in baseball, football and track, reportedly running the 100-yard dash in 10.0 on a dirt track in tennis shoes. At Montana, after serving four years in the Navy, he nearly qualified for the Olympic Trials in the 440, missing by two-tenths of a second. In 1959, Granbois won the Grizzly Cup as the university's outstanding athlete. Poplar's football and track facility was named in Granbois' honor in 2003. Granbois went on to become a coach, teacher and athletic director in Poplar for 24 years, retiring in 1985. Thomas "Mike" Granbois died in 2001 in Poplar.

Powderville

TY O'CONNOR

FOOTBALL

An eastern Montana rancher through and through, O'Connor was yet another small-town star who made it big in college—in his case Montana State. A defensive lineman, he was an honorable mention All-American in 1997 and first-team a year later. At Plevna High School, he was a standout in football and basketball. In 1994, he was Montana's Gatorade Circle of Champions Player of the Year. Thought to have a shot at the pros, O'Connor instead opted to return to the family's 100% organic crops and cattle ranch near Powderville, where he has raised a family and founded the Leaders, Legends and Legacies Football Camp staged each summer, initially in Ekalaka and later in Belgrade.

Power

JACQUE MELLINGER

TRACK AND FIELD

From 2003-06, Mellinger was the top pole vaulter in the Montana, winning three state championships in four years. Mellinger also excelled in the shot put and sprints, and competed in both the pole vault and 100-meter dash at the University of Hawaii. Before high school, Mellinger also was a standout in club gymnastics, routinely competing for gold on the uneven parallel bars, balance beam and in the all-around in invitational meets across the state. A native of Great Falls, Mellinger also was academic all-state.

Pray

CONNOR WINES

FOOTBALL

A star at Gardiner, Wines commuted from the family ranch in Pray, where he has lived the cowboy life and participated in rodeo. In high school, he was an all-round athlete for Gardiner, where he was one of the Bruins' top scorers as a basketball player and twice earned all-district honors. In football, he was all-state at quarterback and linebacker, rushing for 1,374 yards and 18 TDs as a senior. Wines went on to Montana Tech, where he has been one of the top players in the Frontier Conference as a linebacker. He earned first-team all-conference honors in 2018.

Pryor

EYMARD LEFTHAND

BASKETBALL

The right-handed Lefthand could score from anywhere and led the nearby school of Edgar to the Class C state championship in 1966—becoming the first predominantly Crow Indian team to win a crown in Montana. Lefthand, who grew up just outside of Pryor, scored 70 points in Edgar's three wins, earning MVP honors for the tournament. He scored 1,846 points in his four-year career at Edgar. He averaged 22.4 points as a senior and 20.6 as a junior, securing a basketball scholarship to Eastern Montana College. Also a football star in high school, Lefthand later coached at Plenty Coups and St. Labre. He died at home in Pryor in July 2020.

Radersburg

LARRY DUFF

BASEBALL

Radersburg isn't much—a once-booming mining town now with 66 residents—but it has some pop on the national stage. Actress Myrna Loy was born there in 1905 and then there was Cecil "Larry" Duff, who was born in 1896 and had a cup of coffee as a pitcher with the Chicago White Sox in 1922. Three years after the infamous Black Sox Scandal, Duff pitched in three games for Chicago, fashioning a 1-1 record with a save and 4.97 earned-run average. He died in Bend, Oregon, in 1969.

Ramsay

RON UELAND

FOOTBALL

Born and raised on a ranch, Ueland starred in football and track at Butte Central High School, then moved on to play football at Montana State. Nicknamed "Country" because of his rural upbringing, he is widely considered to be the greatest Butte Central lineman ever, anchoring a 1969 team that ran for a school-record 2,788 yards (309 per game). Sonny Holland and Bob Petrino each called Ueland the best player they ever coached. As a Bobcat, he was a captain, earned all-Big Sky Conference honors twice as a linebacker, and was honorable mention All-America in 1973. Ueland was inducted into MSU's Hall of Fame in 1999. After college, Ueland built a multi-billion-dollar agrichemical business for ConAgra before returning to Montana to found two seed companies. Ueland died in May 2018.

Rapelje

JOSH DANNENBERG

BASKETBALL

A high-scoring guard, Dannenberg led Rapelje to its first District 5C championship in 30 years in 1991, averaging more than 27 points over three games and hitting the game-winning shot to beat top-ranked Melstone. He routinely scored more than 30 points in games. Dannenberg also was a solid track athlete, placing for Rapelje in the hurdles at the state meet. He continued his basketball career at Western Montana. Dannenberg is a sales executive in the Billings area today.

Red Lodge

ALICE GREENOUGH (ORR)

RODEO

Often called the "Queen of Rodeo," Greenough performed in rodeos across the country, including Madison Square Garden in New York, and was renowned internationally for both bull riding and trick riding. She was so popular she was once ranked among the "100 Most Influential Montanans of the Century." She began bronc riding in 1929 and joined the PRCA in 1936. After retiring from riding, she did occasional work in movies and for the NBC show *Little House on the Prairie*. She has been inducted into numerous Halls of Fame, including the National Cowboy and Western Heritage Hall of Fame, and she was the first person to be enshrined in the National Cowgirl Museum and Hall of Fame. Greenough died at her home in Tucson, Arizona, in 1995.

Reed Point

ELLY BRUURSEMA

BASKETBALL

A star of the public-television documentary *Class C*, Bruursema led Reed Point to state titles in 2005 and '06 and remains fifth on Montana's all-time career scoring list with 2,221 points. She scored 48 points in a single game in her senior season and ranks third in state history with 51 games of 20 points or more. A three-time all-stater and 2006 Montana Gatorade Player of the Year winner, Bruursema went on to play for Carroll College, where she was one of the Frontier Conference's top 3-point shooters, was co-freshman of the year and earned first-team all-conference honors. Bruursema is a physical therapist in Belgrade.

Richey

JIM SOFT

BASKETBALL

An outstanding athlete in four sports, Soft was Montana's second-leading scorer his senior basketball season at Richey. He excelled beyond high school in basketball, though, becoming a two-time All-American and Frontier Conference Player of the year in 1968 for Eastern Montana College. He played four positions in football and qualified for the state track meet in eight events. As a senior for Richey, Soft averaged 20 rebounds per game. His No. 50 was retired by EMC and he is in the school's Hall of Fame. After college, he played for Athletes In Action. Soft's older brother Loren, an all-conference football player on offense and defense for EMC, was an exceptional athlete as well, earning an NFL shot with the Baltimore Colts. Jim Soft was president of the Yellowstone Boys & Girls Ranch Foundation from 2002-12 and continues to support an organization with which he began working in 1972.

Roberts

CARSON DURR

BASKETBALL

The sharp-shooting wing averaged 22.1 points and 10.5 rebounds in leading the Rockets to the Class C state tournament in 2001-02. His 48 games with 20 or more points for his career are tied for seventh in state history. Durr was a first-team all-state quarterback in football and was first-team all-conference as a kicker, punter and linebacker. He also set the Class C record in the javelin in 2002 with a toss of 171-11. Durr continued his basketball career at Montana State, where he was all-academic for four years. Today, Durr is a chiropractor with offices in Bozeman and Gardiner.

Rocky Boy

DONNIE PARISIAN

BASKETBALL

Though from Rocky Boy, Parisian played high school ball in Heart Butte, where he averaged 23 points and 15 rebounds as a senior in 1993. He went on to a stellar collegiate career at Montana State-Northern, where as a center he earned second-team Frontier Conference honors as a senior. He averaged 13.1 points and 6.3 rebounds per game in leading the Lights to the NAIA national tournament in Kansas City in 1998. Along the way, he had some big games, scoring 30 points and grabbing 13 rebounds in a win over Rocky Mountain College. Parisian started his college career at Miles Community College. He has worked for Cemex for the past two decades, most recently as a production coordinator in the Los Angeles area.

Ronan

MARVIN CAMEL BOXING

One of 13 children who grew up on the Flathead Reservation, Camel made his boxing debut at age 12 and eventually became the greatest fighter the state has ever known. In 1980, the southpaw won the World Boxing Council's cruiserweight title and in 1983 became the International Boxing Federation's first champion, making him the first in his class to be recognized as world champion by two sanctioning bodies. He's also the first Native American to be a world champ. In 2006, Camel was awarded honorary champion status by the WBC. In 62 professional fights, Camel won 45—21 of them by knockout. He was 140-40 as an amateur. In high school, Camel set a school record in the 880-yard run. In 2007, he was inducted into the Montana Indian Athletic Hall of Fame. He now lives in Tavares, Florida, where he runs a lawn care business and teaches boxing.

Roscoe

CLINT BRANGER

BULL RIDING

Long considered one of the top bull riders in the world, Branger was a founding member of the Professional Bull Riders (PBR). A 1983 Absarokee High graduate, he was a collegiate national champion at Northwest College in Wyoming and earned the first of his eight NFR qualifications in 1987. He finished third in the PRCA standings in 1990 and 1992, and led the PBR standings for most of 1994. Brangar retired from bull riding at age 36 in 2000. He still lives on a ranch outside of Roscoe.

Rosebud

BRAC WARREN

BASEBALL

A native of Rosebud, where his parents still live, Warren went on to pitch for the Miles City Outlaws and graduated from high school in Miles City in 2014. He then pitched for the University of Oregon, where after three years his 97 mph fastball and assortment of pitches caught the eye of the San Francisco Giants. He was drafted in the 17th round in 2017 and made his pro debut in August 2019 after two years of injuries. The Giants released him in June 2020. Warren also was an all-conference basketball player for Miles City.

Roundup

SHANE COLLINS

FOOTBALL

An eventual all-stater at Bozeman High and national Gatorade Athlete of the Year in both football and track and field in 1986-87, Collins was a dominant defensive lineman at Arizona State—earning all-conference honors three times—and also was the national shot put champion for ASU, where the Roundup native is in the Hall of Fame. Collins, called "The Natural" in a story by *The Sporting News*, was a six-time All-American in track for the Sun Devils. In 1992, the Washington Redskins drafted him in the second round, and he played three seasons in the NFL. Collins also was a three-year starter in basketball for Bozeman, averaging 17 points and 12 rebounds a game en route to earning first-team all-state honors for the second consecutive season in 1987. He is in the Montana Football Hall of Fame. After his football career ended, Collins returned to Bozeman, where he owns Shane Collins Construction.

Roy

FLOYD EMERY

TRACK AND FIELD

A champion sprinter, Emery routinely set records in the 100, 200 and both hurdles events in the early 1950s. It wasn't unusual for Emery to accumulate at least 20 points per meet, even at divisionals. Emery also was a key player on the Pirates' basketball and football teams. An accomplished archer as well, Emery died in 2018 after a life in farming.

Rudyard

TODD ANDERSON

BASKETBALL

In a town famed for its "596 nice people—One Old Sore Head," Anderson is arguably its nicest all-round athlete. A prolific scorer, he was the basketball team's leading scorer in 1978, first-team all-state in 1979 and the top rebounder in the Class C tournament.

Ryegate

JOHN WRZESINSKI

RODEO

The name is familiar on the Montana sporting landscape, and it was John Wrzesinski who started it all, winning College National Finals Rodeo titles for Rocky Mountain College in 1961 and '62 before snagging the '64 Montana Rodeo Association all-around crown. A champion saddle bronc rider and steer wrestler, Wrzesinski also competed on the European Rodeo Tour. He was inducted into the Montana Pro Rodeo Hall & Wall of Fame in 2015. Wrzesinski was among the first 10 Montanans to appear in *Sports Illustrated*'s "Faces In The Crowd" after winning the all-around cowboy award at the Montana State Rodeo. At Ryegate, where he was a standout basketball player, he became a school teacher while competing in rodeo. He lives in Harlowton.

St. Ignatius

J.R. CAMEL

BASKETBALL

For three years, Camel starred on the court for Mission before transferring to Missoula Hellgate, where he averaged 23 points per game and led the Knights to an unbeaten championship season in 1992-93 en route to earning Montana Gatorade Player of the Year honors. He was Big Sky Conference freshman of the year at Montana, set the school's career record for steals, and was all-conference his sophomore and junior years. After forgoing his senior season after the birth of a daughter, Camel played professionally for three years in what was then Yugoslavia before returning to the Flathead Reservation to coach. He still ranks eighth in career assists for UM. Camel later coached the boys basketball team at Arlee and then at Salish Kootenai College. He is in the Montana Indian Athletic Hall of Fame.

St. Marie

ROY ROBINSON

TRACK AND FIELD

The son of an Air Force sergeant, Robinson just might be the greatest track and field athlete in state history. The 1966 Glasgow High grad was the high scorer at three consecutive state meets, becoming the first Montanan to accomplish the feat, and overall won 15 individual titles. Along the way he won four consecutive 100-yard dash titles, three in the 180- and 220-yard low hurdles, and added two wins in the 120 hurdles. Oh, and he was a four-year starter for the Scotties in football. Robinson was a star in both sports at Montana, winning Big Sky titles in the 100 and high hurdles. He is enshrined in the school's Hall of Fame for both sports. An inductee in the inaugural MHSA Athletes' Hall of Fame class, he earned shots with the Atlanta Falcons and Denver Broncos of the NFL, played a season with the Saskatchewan Roughriders of the CFL, and had a tryout with Portland of the World Football League before retiring. Robinson lives in Missoula.

St. Regis

JOE NIESLANIK

TRACK AND FIELD

A three-sport standout, Nieslanik shined most in track, where he was one of the state's best in the pole vault and triple jump in the late 1970s and 1980. In 1980, he set meet records in the triple jump and pole vault at the Western C meet, and was the state Class C pole vault champ with a leap of 13-0. He also was one of the school's top football players and in basketball Nieslanik was an honorable mention all-stater in 1980. Nieslanik attended Northern Colorado and now is an account executive for an insurance agency in Portland, Oregon.

St. Xavier

TUFF HARRIS

FOOTBALL

Nicknamed "Tuff" because he survived pneumonia as a newborn, Chester Harris earned his high school acclaim at Colstrip, where he competed in football, basketball and track—setting the all-class state record in the 100-meter dash as a junior in 2001 and winning seven individual state crowns overall. Recruited to run track at Montana, he walked on as a football player and became a four-year starter at cornerback, also setting school and conference records for most punt return yards in a game and season. Signed as an undrafted free agent, Harris would go on to play for five NFL teams over five seasons and also had a stint with the Edmonton Eskimos of the CFL. He was inducted into the Montana Indian Athletic Hall of Fame in 2018 and also is in the Montana Football Hall of Fame. Today, Harris—part Crow and part Northern Cheyenne—has poured himself into Native American issues with his "One Heart Warriors" program.

Saco

ROCKY TOLLEFSON

BASKETBALL

The son of a farmer, "Rockland" Tollefson led Saco to the 1971 state championship game against Busby and finished his career with 2,326 points—a career record for Montana until the 3-point line came along. After high school, he accepted a basketball scholarship at Montana State, where he played in 32 games. He eventually became a basketball coach in Malta. He died of cancer in 2005 at age 52.

Sand Coulee

TERRY ADKINS

MUSHER

In a community notable for numerous mushers, Adkins is the preeminent name among them. A Kentucky native who came to Montana via the Air Force, he ran his first Iditarod in Alaska in 1974 and has since run it 22 times. Adkins also was the Iditarod's lone veterinarian in its 1973 debut. He is a fixture in Montana's annual Race to the Sky.

Sand Springs

BILL BROWN

RODEO

A native of Texas, the 1953 Northwest Ranch Cowboys Association calf roping champion lived most of his adult life at his ranch outside of Sand Springs. While at the University of Wyoming, he was student body president in 1952 and a major player in the creation of the National Intercollegiate Rodeo Association. Soon after, the native of Sheridan, Wyoming, moved to a ranch near Birney and eventually to another ranch 11 miles from Sand Springs where they ran cattle. Brown, who was president of the Montana Stockgrowers Association for two years, died in 2012.

Savage

RYDER RICE

FOOTBALL

A first-team all-stater on the defensive line for the Warriors, Rice was the MVP of two all-star games in the summer of 2015 before continuing his football career at Rocky Mountain College. By his junior year in 2018, he was a second-team NAIA All-American after recording 56 tackles, 17 for losses; his 12.5 sacks were sixth nationally. Rice opted to finish his college career at Montana in 2019. He also led Savage's basketball team in assists and steals, and he was district pole vault champion.

Scobey

SPENCER FREDERICK

FOOTBALL

The definition of a champion, Frederick was an all-purpose star who led the Spartans to unbeaten 8-Man football seasons and state titles in 1995-96. Not to be outdone, in basketball he scored 22 points and had 12 rebounds to lead Scobey to the Class C title in 1995-96, beating Gardiner 70-38 to set a record for victory margin in a title game. Frederick went on to play for Montana's 2001 national championship football team. He was an all-Big Sky tight end that same year and earned a shot with the New Orleans Saints of the NFL before injuries ended his career. Frederick returned to Montana and became a vice president at Billings' downtown Stockman Bank branch.

Seeley Lake

LES MEYER

FOOTBALL

A standout athlete in high school, Meyer went on to a solid four-year football career at Rocky Mountain College. At Seeley Lake, he was a star running back on the football team, played basketball and was a sprinter and hurdler in track. But it's what he's done since that's perhaps more impressive, building Fairfield into one of the state's Class B football powerhouses as a coach. After starting his coaching career as an assistant in 1993, four years later Meyer started at Fairfield and 20 years after that was a finalist for national coach of the year. In early 2020, Meyer left Fairfield to become superintendent at Frenchtown.

Seville

SAM BIRD JR.

RODEO

The nephew of the revered Blackfeet basketball player Samson Bird, Sam was one of the great team ropers in Montana history, winning his first buckle at age 12 with the legendary Bud Connelly. A header, Bird won a world championship at the Indian National Finals Rodeo in 1976. He won two more world championships in the next 25 years, including with his nephew, Dustin, a three-time NFR qualifier. In addition to his successes in Indian rodeos, Bird was a seven-time Montana Pro Rodeo team roping champion and also a two-time Northern Rodeo Association team-roping winner. He was inducted into the Montana Indian Athletic Hall of Fame in 2008 and the Montana Pro Rodeo Hall of Fame in 2013.

Shelby

LARRY KRYSTKOWIAK

BASKETBALL

Though a graduate of Big Sky High in Missoula, Krystkowiak was Shelby-born and spent most of his formative years on the Hi-Line, where his basketball prowess began to blossom. Highly recruited, he stayed home and became arguably the greatest player in Montana Griz history, setting school records for points (2,017) and rebounds (1,105). A two-time academic all-American, Krystkowiak is the only player in Big Sky history to win three league MVP awards. He would go on to play 11 seasons in the NBA with six teams, retiring in 1997 to become a coach. "Krysko" coached his alma mater for two seasons, did another year in the NBA with the Milwaukee Bucks, and has been head coach at the University of Utah since 2011. Krystkowiak's No. 42 jersey has been retired by UM. He is enshrined in the National Polish-American Hall of Fame and the Grizzly Sports Hall of Fame.

Shepherd

EMMETT WILLSON

WRESTLING

One of the greatest wrestlers in state history, Wilson stands alone for one feat—winning the 2004 Dan Hodge Trophy, awarded to the nation's top collegiate wrestler in any class. He won three national championships for MSU-Northern and was a four-time NAIA All-American, but in 2004 he went 50-0—with 24 pins—and topped eight NCAA qualifiers, including the wrestlers who finished third and fourth. He was the first NAIA wrestler to win the Hodge Trophy. Willson, a two-time state champion at Shepherd, finished his career with a 163-16 record. He was inducted into the MSU-Northern Hall of Fame in 2014 and the NAIA Hall of Fame three years later.

Sheridan

MARK KIECKBUSCH

TRACK AND FIELD

An all-round star in three sports, Kieckbusch won the 400- and 800-meter state championships and led the Panthers to three consecutive state track and field championships (1984-86). In 1986, he set a district record in the 400, and he was on two Panthers relay teams that owned longstanding Class C state records. Part of a notable Sheridan athletic family, Kieckbusch also was the quarterback of the football team and a starting point guard in basketball. He later co-coached the Billings Little League team that advanced to the World Series in 2011. An electrical engineer, Kieckbusch works in Billings as a senior project engineer.

Shonkin

CHRIS DIEKHANS

FOOTBALL

Raised in the lake country between Geraldine and Highwood, Diekhans was a 6-Man all-stater in football, an all-conference basketball player and a standout in the hurdles and sprints for Geraldine's track team. Despite playing with a broken bone in his wrist, he ran for two touchdowns to lead the Tigers to the 1989 state 6-Man football championship with a 23-6 victory over Denton. Diekhans continued his athletic career at the University of Mary, where he was a defensive back in football and also ran track. He returned to the Golden Triangle to work in the cattle and ag industry.

Sidney

DEB PREVOST

BASKETBALL

A trail blazer in every way, Prevost was a point guard on Sidney's first girls basketball team in 1973, walked on at Eastern Montana College and became an All-American. In 1978, she was drafted by the Minnesota Fillies of the brand-new Women's Professional Basketball League, where she earned Player of the Week honors a year later with the Milwaukee Does. After the league folded, Prevost returned to Sidney for a long teaching career. In 2018, she was honored by the Women's Basketball Hall of Fame in Knoxville, Tennessee, as a "trailblazer of the game." Prevost is now retired from teaching but is a grief recovery specialist in Sidney.

Simms

GARY AND DAVE GUSTAFSON

FOOTBALL/BASKETBALL

Gustafson is a big sports name in the Golden Triangle, but none quite match Gary and Dave. Gary is one of the great defensive linemen to come out of Montana. A two-sport standout, he competed three times in the National High School Rodeo Finals. After dominating in high school football, he went to Montana State, where he became the program's first All-American on the defensive line in 1969. He was inducted into MSU's Athletic Hall of Fame in 2006. Also a two-sport standout, Dave was right there with him, starring at guard on the UM basketball team in the late 1960s. He was first-team all-Big Sky and finished second in the league in scoring to Idaho State's prolific Willie Humes in 1970. Dave, who held numerous school records at Simms, also was a solid javelin thrower for the track team. In 1979, he was inducted into UM's Sports Hall of Fame. Gary eventually moved to a family ranch near Jeffers in the Madison Valley. Dave died in a plane crash in 1986.

Square Butte

JAN MAYO (WISHMAN)

TRACK AND FIELD

Also a standout basketball player at Geraldine, Mayo was the Class C state champion in the 300 hurdles in 1985 then set state marks in the 100 hurdles and 300 hurdles in '86. A week later, she won the 100, 200 and 300 hurdles at the 1986 Montana Track and Field Meet of Champions and was subsequently invited to represent the United States on a Northwest Track and Field Camp team touring Europe. Mayo is ranching near Geraldine.

Stanford

JON WRZESINSKI

TRACK AND FIELD

Wrzesinski was all-state in three sports. He was a two-time state champion and Class C record-holder in the pole vault and he was twice a state runner-up and once a third-place finisher in wrestling. Wrzesinski kept rolling in two sports at the North Dakota State College of Sciences, where he was an all-conference quarterback and an all-American in track, finishing second at the national junior college meet in the decathlon. He continued his collegiate career at North Dakota in both sports, earning all-league honors as a wide receiver in 1987. To cap it off, Wrzesinski was an all-American in the pole vault and decathlon, and still holds the UND school record in the decathlon. After college, he coached briefly at Mary before moving to Asia for 10 years and returning to Montana to be a principal and superintendent. He was hired as Hardin's superintendent in August 2020.

Stevensville

JOE CUMMINGS

FOOTBALL

The son of an NFL player and Stanford Hall of Famer (Ed Cummings), Joe was Montana's all-class player of the year for Stevi in 1991 and earned a scholarship to play linebacker for Wyoming. By the time his career was over, he was a first-team all-Western Athletic Conference selection and was signed as an undrafted free agent by the Philadelphia Eagles. Thus began a six-year career as a journeyman linebacker. In 2000, Cummings returned to Wyoming to finish his degree, played briefly in the new XFL, and finally returned home to the Bitterroot Valley to work as a fishing guide.

Stockett

JEFF SHIRLEY

FOOTBALL

An iron man if there ever was one, Shirley was a two-way player who led Centerville to its first 8-Man state football championship in 1999. For college, he chose Carroll, where he was a first-team NAIA All-American and played in a national record 58 consecutive games while winning four consecutive national titles. As a senior with the Saints, he was Frontier Conference Defensive Player of the Year. In 2009, Shirley was chosen to the NAIA All-Decade second team and seven years later was inducted into Carroll's Hall of Fame. Shirley owns a physical therapy practice in Helena.

Sula

HAL WETZSTEON

BASEBALL

Raised on a homestead just outside of Sula, Wetzsteon was a four-sport athlete at Darby in the mid-1950s before moving on to star at Western Montana College. He was a standout first baseman on the baseball team and also played basketball for the Bulldogs. Behind his pitching, Western won the 1959 conference championship. Wetzsteon left Western a year early to return to the family ranch after his father was injured. Eventually he worked for the Forest Service in Wisdom as an incident commander and fire management officer. He was inducted into Montana Western's Hall of Fame in 1995. Wetzsteon died in 2007 in Dillon, where he had worked in law enforcement.

Photo: Hal Wetzsteon, back row, third from right.

Sun River

TIM LOWRY

FOOTBALL

Lowry was big man on campus—literally—for nearby Simms High School, where he was a standout in football as a lineman and an imposing basketball center from 1987-91. From Simms, he matriculated at Concordia (Minn.) University, where he was all-MIAC and eventually became a first-team All-American in 1995 after leading the Cobbers to a league championship. Lowry was enshrined in Concordia's Hall of Fame in 2015. After college, he founded a concrete company in Spokane, Washington, and lives in northern Idaho.

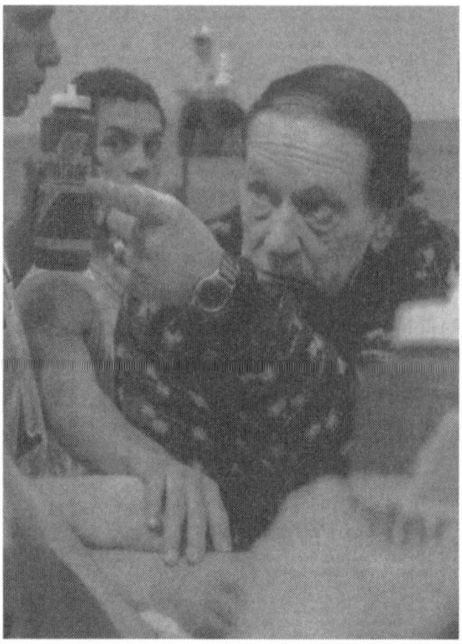

Sunburst

KIM L. HAINES

BASKETBALL/TRACK

A native of Havre, Haines was a rarity—a letter-winner in five sports for the Refiners—and the only athlete in this entire book to include badminton on his resume. He also lettered in track, basketball, football and baseball. After starting in college at Montana, he transferred to Northern Montana College, where he was all-conference in basketball for two years and led the Lights into the NAIA tournament in the early 1950s. Haines also took a shot at the Olympics in track. After his competitive career ended, he went into coaching at a variety of high schools, including 37 years at Seeley-Swan—amassing a state-record 670 wins in basketball, a mark that still ranks second—and started the Western Montana Track Club. He was inducted into the Montana Coaches Hall of Fame in 1992 and MSU-Northern's Athletic Hall of Fame in 1998. Haines died in 2013.

Superior

POKEY ALLEN

FOOTBALL

Though best remembered for his high school years in Missoula, the first five years of this legendary athlete and coach's life were spent downstream on the Clark Fork River. The son of a Montana Highway Patrol officer, Allen was a star in football, basketball and track at Missoula County High School before moving on to play quarterback at Utah. As a defensive player in 1964, he was MVP of the Liberty Bowl. He then played three seasons in the Canadian Football League before embarking on a Hall of Fame coaching career in 1968. After three seasons as an assistant at Montana, he became a head coach at Portland State and then Boise State, where in his second season (1994) he took the Broncos to the NCAA Division I-AA title game, where they lost to Youngstown State. Two days later, he was diagnosed with a rare form of cancer and in December 1996 he died in Missoula. A book—*Pokey: The Good Fight*—was written posthumously by Boise author Bob Evancho.

Terry

LACEY HAUGHIAN

BASKETBALL

Among Terry's greats, Haughian stands above the rest—literally. The 6-foot-2 forward/center dominated for the Terriers in high school and built on her success at Black Hills State in South Dakota, where she was a first-team NAIA All-American in 2008. Haughian led the Yellowjackets to the Elite 8 at the national tournament and ranks fifth all-time in scoring for the school (1,417 points). After college, she played professionally overseas—first in Sweden, then in Denmark and finally in Germany. Haughian also was a standout volleyball player and state champion javelin thrower in high school. She twice placed at the NAIA national track meet for Black Hills State. Today, she runs a cattle ranch near Terry and works as a BLM ranger in the summers.

Thompson Falls

DON HEATER

FOOTBALL

At a school that has produced its share of top-flight football players, Heater shines not just for his exceptional high school career but for what he did later. At Montana Tech from 1968-71, he led the nation in touchdowns and yards rushing, set a national mark for carries in a season and set longstanding school records for yards rushing in a single game, season and career (4,385)—the latter mark lasting 44 years. Heater's 1,797 yards in 1971 were an NAIA record for 13 years, and he is still Tech's leading career scorer. The "Rambling Wreck from Tech" was chosen Montana Athlete of the Year, was two-time Frontier Conference Player of the Year and was the Frontier's first NAIA All-American in 1971. He played two games for the St. Louis Cardinals of the NFL in 1972. Heater was an exceptional all-round athlete for Thompson Falls, fashioning the highest single-game scoring output in Western B basketball in 1968. He is enshrined in Montana Tech's Hall of Fame. He works for a multi-national mining company in Azerbaijan.

Three Forks

MICK DURHAM

BASKETBALL

A scrappy point guard, Durham led Three Forks to the 1974 Class B state title and edges MSU Hall of Famer Vicki Heebner (Carle) as the Wolves' top all-time athlete. He went on to become one of the most prominent names on Montana's basketball landscape. He was ranked second in assists and free-throw percentage when he left Montana State in 1980; he remains fourth in both categories. After playing for MSU, he coached the Bobcats to their last Big Sky Conference championship in 1996 and was the league's coach of the year three times. He briefly left the business, returned as an assistant at New Mexico State and then guided the program at Alaska Fairbanks before returning home to lead the men's program at MSU Billings.

Toston

JOANNE SLIFKA

BASKETBALL

Slifka was a multi-sport star in the late 1970s for Townsend, where she was a four-year letter winner and two-time team MVP in basketball. She took her gifts to Montana Western, where she was a champion in the 800 meters on the track and a four-time all-conference basketball performer as a center. She also was an honors student and Western's third female student body president when elected in 1981. Also a Miss Townsend Rodeo in 1979 and a contestant for Miss Rodeo Montana, Slifka was inducted into the Montana Western Hall of Fame in 1992. After college, she became a teacher and a coach. Slifka now works with the Alturas International Academy, a public charter school in Idaho Falls, Idaho.

Townsend

JADE RAUSER

WRESTLING

One of the state's all-time greats, from the moment he stepped on the mat as a freshman Rauser embarked on a winning streak that'll be tough to top. By the time he was done at Broadwater High in 2011, he was a four-time state B-C champion with a 175-0 record—shattering the previous record for consecutive wins in the process after becoming the third wrestler in state history to start 100-0. Rauser also won a gold medal in the Pan Am Games and took national crowns in Greco-Roman, freestyle and folkstyle. He took his wrestling prowess to Utah Valley University, where he was a four-time NCAA qualifier, finished third at the Big 12 tournament and was an All-American in his senior year (2016). His 77 career wins for the Wolverines rank fifth in program history. After his career, Rauser took over as director of operations for Utah Valley's wrestling program and also became a youth development coach for USA Wrestling Utah.

Troy

BLAINE MCELMURRY

FOOTBALL

A do-everything standout athlete at Troy, McElmurry made his presence felt most on the football field, where he was an all-state quarterback and defensive back for the Trojans. His game-winning touchdown pass in overtime gave Troy a 22-14 upset win over top-ranked Cut Bank for the 1991 Class B state championship. McElmurry also was all-state in basketball and a state champion in the long jump and triple jump. He was even better as a free safety for Montana, earning All-America and Academic All-America honors. He went undrafted but made the Green Bay Packers as a rookie in 1997, with the potential of becoming the first Montanan to win a high school state title, college national title (1995) and a Super Bowl ring—until the Packers lost to Denver. McElmurry bounced around with several NFL teams before his five-year career ended. Since 2003 he has owned a custom home construction business in Missoula.

Turner

CHERYL AND JULIANN KELLER

BASKETBALL

A sister act and part of the Lady Griz pipeline from Malta, the Kellers grew up three years apart on a wheat farm outside of Turner as part of an athletic family that sent five siblings into college athletics. The older of the two, Cheryl averaged 17 points and six rebounds per game in leading the M'ettes to a Class B state title as a senior in 1997. Cheryl led Montana in scoring and was an all-Big Sky guard her senior year in 2002 despite a painful shin injury. Juliann was even more of a threat on the hoop court in high school, averaging nearly 22 points and eight rebounds as a senior before joining her sister in Missoula, earning Montana Gatorade Player of the Year honors. As a senior, Juliann averaged nearly 16 points a game in conference play. The two played together at UM in 2001-02 and were the only sisters to play for legendary coach Robin Selvig on the same team. Juliann coached in Kentucky, was an assistant women's basketball coach at MSU-Northern and now teaches in East Helena. Cheryl lives in Las Vegas and is married to Deldre Carr, a former UM basketball player who is a college basketball referee.

Twin Bridges

PEYTON FERRIS

BASKETBALL

The 5-foot-9 post was a four-time all-state basketball selection for Twin Bridges and averaged 18.2 points and 7.1 rebounds as a senior in leading the Falcons to the state title game. Also a standout in volleyball, Ferris was Montana's Gatorade Player of the Year in 2011-12 and scored 41 points in a Class C state championship game loss to Belt. Ferris went on to become the 11th-leading scorer in Montana State history and earned Big Sky MVP honors in 2017, becoming the 12th player in school history to score 1,000 points and grab 500 rebounds. Ferris now plays professionally in Spain.

Two Dot

JASON CARLSON

RODEO

The little ranching town on the Musselshell River—immortalized by country legend Hank Williams Jr.—doesn't have a prodigious athletic history, but Carlson has done his part on the Montana Pro Rodeo Circuit over the past decade. Carlson continues a solid career as a team roping header. Before that, he was accomplished in track and field at Harlowton, where he was a district champion in the shot put and competitive in the discus in 2006, and an all-conference football player as a center.

Ulm

ROB POLICH

BASKETBALL

Polich, who grew up on a ranch outside of Ulm, was an all-star for Cascade in 1974, when the 6-foot-5 forward set the Northern B divisional record for scoring with 27 points in a game. Polich took his game to Northern Montana College, where he was the team's top scorer in 1978 with a 17 points per game average to earn second-team all-Frontier Conference honors. After his college career, he had a tryout with the Montana Sky semi-professional team in Great Falls. Polich still lives in Ulm.

Valier

SCOTT CURRY

FOOTBALL

Born in Conrad on Christmas Day 1975, Curry was a gift to Valier High School, the University of Montana and—for five games in 1999—as an offensive lineman for the Green Bay Packers of the NFL, who chose him in the sixth round. A first-team all-Big Sky selection who played on Montana's 1995 national championship team, Curry was UM's second Class C player ever to be drafted by an NFL team. He was a left tackle for four years at UM. Curry, an outstanding high school basketball player and track athlete as well, returned home to Valier after retiring from football to run the town's only grocery store.

Vaughn

JOHNNY COUCH

BASEBALL

Born in 1891, Couch pitched for Stanford University, fought in World War I, and then joined the Detroit Tigers in 1917. In 1923, he won 16 games with the Cincinnati Reds and Philadelphia Phillies. Overall, he finished with a 29-34 record in the majors. According to the book *Montana Baseball History*, Couch was proud of his heritage and described himself as an "ex-Montana cowpuncher." He left Montana for California at age 11, but his family maintained ownership of a large ranch near Sun River. Among his feats was striking out Babe Ruth and Ty Cobb. Known as the "gentleman scholar" because he attended Stanford at a time when baseball players weren't well-educated, Couch died in 1975 in Palo Alto, California.

Victor

ROD LYMAN

RODEO

Though he didn't win a world championship, Lyman is one of the sport's most successful competitors. He has earned more than $1.5 million and qualified for 16 NFRs as a steer wrestler. Were it not for rodeo, Lyman might've made money playing football. The Great Falls native traded football for rodeo after a year on the defensive line at Montana State and competed on the Bobcats' rodeo team, earning a berth in the College National Finals Rodeo. Lyman was in the lead for a gold buckle on the final day of the National Finals Rodeo in 1994. He is in the Ellensburg (Wash.) Rodeo Hall of Fame. After retiring in 2008, Lyman spent time between Belgrade and Wickenburg, Arizona, training quarterhorses.

Vida

LISA SCHILLINGER (LOCKHART)

RODEO

Still active, Lockhart is a two-time Wrangler National Finals Rodeo barrel racing champion (2014, 2016) and is a 14-time NFR qualifier. She ranks second all-time on the Women's Professional Rodeo Circuit career money list with more than $2.5 million in earnings. Lockhart—who was born in Wolf Point, attended Circle High School but has always called herself "a Vida girl"—has won over $1 million at the NFR alone. Now a resident of Oelrichs, South Dakota, she has finished among the top five in the world standings eight times, including runner-up in 2014 and 2015 as well as third in 2019.

Volborg

JESS LOCKWOOD

BULL RIDING

Talk about bucking the odds—Lockwood needed only 18 months on the PBR circuit to win his first world championship, in 2017 becoming the youngest (age 20) ever to take the title. And then he did it again in 2019 to become the youngest to win two world championships. A state-champion wrestler at 98 pounds for Broadus in 2013, Lockwood won two Northern Rodeo Association championships and three Montana high school crowns before turning pro on his 18th birthday. He was PBR Rookie of the Year in 2016. In high school in Broadus, Lockwood was a three-time state champion and three times nearly won national titles. Lockwood was injured for much of the 2020 season.

Westby

ALLAN NIELSEN

BASKETBALL

Even before co-oping with neighboring Grenora, North Dakota, Westby was an Eastern C power and Nielsen was a catalyst. He was all-state and Class C tournament MVP in 1975 in leading his team to the state championship win over Antelope, averaging 32.3 points and 18.7 rebounds per game. Nielsen then was a second-team all-Big Sky honoree his junior and senior years at Montana, where he was the team MVP as a senior. He was inducted into the school's Hall of Fame and his jersey retired in 1980, a year after he died in a road construction accident on Interstate 90 west of St. Regis the summer after college. The Grizzlies each year give an Allan Nielsen Award to the player who "best represents Griz basketball."

West Yellowstone

BAILEE PARKER

CROSS COUNTRY

Parker was a four-sport athlete and earned 13 letters with the Wolverines, excelling in basketball, track, cross country, and volleyball in a career that concluded in 2016. She was a four-time state champion in the 3,200 and three-time champ in the 800 and 1,600. Splitting time between volleyball and cross country in the fall, Parker was a two-time state champion in cross country. Her running exploits took her to Utah State, where she already ranks seventh in school history in the 5,000 meters indoors, 10th outdoors in the 3,000 and for a brief time was ninth outdoors in the 5,000. Parker did not compete as a junior in the 2019 cross country and indoor season due to an injury.

White Pine

GARY COOPER

BASKETBALL

Cooper was a star down the road at Thompson Falls, where he was an all-state basketball player. He elevated his game at Western Montana College from 1955-59, earning all-conference and all-district honors four consecutive seasons. Cooper was the Bulldogs' first All-American in 1959 and holds the school scoring record with 2,350 points in his career. After his career ended, he was offered a tryout with the New York Knicks but turned it down to complete his education. Cooper, who would later coach at four high schools and guided the UMW women's program from 1985-93, was enshrined in Western's Hall of Fame in 1981. He is retired and living in Thompson Falls.

White Sulphur Springs

CY WILLIAMS

FOOTBALL

There might not be a more prolific passer in state history than Williams, who is far and away the 8-Man state record holder in career completed passes with 591. His three seasons (2009-11) rank No. 1, No. 4 and No. 5 all-time in completed passes, and he still owns eight of the top 11 single-game marks—his 52 completions against Charlo in 2010 topping them all. Williams' 88 career TD passes also are a state all-class record. Williams, a football all-stater who also played basketball and threw the javelin in high school, went on to play briefly for Montana Tech. An environmental engineer, Williams is a project manager for Missouri River Contractors in Helena.

Whitefish

TOMMY MOE

SKIING

Groomed at The Big Mountain Resort, Moe became one of the nation's greatest Alpine ski racers and spent 12 years on the U.S. team. At the 1994 Winter Olympics, he stunned the world by winning gold in the downhill and silver in the super-giant slalom, the latter on his 24th birthday. A three-time Olympian who made his World Cup debut at age 17, Moe was born in Missoula and lived in Whitefish until moving at age 13 to Alaska, where he trained, has owned a whitewater-rafting guiding service and co-owned a mountain lodge. He won five U.S. Alpine championships and one World Cup Super-G title. Plagued by injuries, he retired after the 1998 Olympics, where he was eighth in the Super-G and 12th in the downhill. Big Mountain's Moe Mentum run is named for him and he is enshrined in the Alaska Hall of Fame.

Whitehall

SHAWN DAVIS

RODEO

Born in Butte, Davis is a rodeo legend, from his days as a three-time world champion saddle bronc rider to his larger imprint on the sport as general manager of the Wrangler National Finals Rodeo from 1986-2019. He won his world titles in 1965, 1967 and 1968, and was leading the world standings in 1969 when he suffered an injury. Before that, he was a college all-around champion at Western Montana College in 1962. Davis, made an honorary member of the Blackfeet Tribe in 1973, might be best known for his deciding vote in moving the NFR in 1985 from Oklahoma City to Las Vegas. A one-hour documentary about Davis called *Cowboy Strong—The Man Behind the NFR Legacy In Vegas* aired on CBS Sports in 2018. He was in the inaugural induction class of the ProRodeo Hall of Fame in 1979 and was deemed a Legend of ProRodeo in 2011.

Whitewater

KRYSTAL SIMONSON

BASKETBALL

A member of a prominent sports family in Whitewater, Simonson averaged 19 points and 12 rebounds a game in her senior season in 1994-95 and was Class C all-state three years in a row. She started all four years, led Whitewater to its first state title game appearance in 1994 and was chosen to play in the 1996 Montana Girls All-Star Basketball Classic. Simonson began her collegiate career at MSU Billings but transferred after one season to Rocky Mountain College, where she was a frequent double-figure scorer. Simonson has been working in marketing in Billings for the past two decades.

Wibaux

TRAVIS BERTELSEN

FOOTBALL

The do-everything player from the 8-Man powerhouse (now 6-Man) stands alone atop the state record books for career total offense with 6,718 yards (2005-08), more than 700 ahead of runner-up Zach Molyneaux of Chinook. Bertelsen's 3,989 career rushing yards are fifth all-time and his 2,272 total yards in 2006 are fourth all-time. His 79 career rushing TDs rank second and his 35 TD receptions are fourth. A three-time all-stater in basketball and a standout in track by the time his high school career wrapped up in 2009, Bertelsen started collegiately at Montana State in football before transferring to Rocky Mountain College. He is an electrician in Billings.

Willard

JACK WESTROPE

HORSE RACING

Born in Baker in 1917, Westrope grew up around horses on a ranch between Ismay and Willard, a small community on MT 7 between Baker and Ekalaka. He began racing professionally in "bush races" on small tracks in eastern Montana and western North Dakota and South Dakota, winning his first race at age 12. As a 15-year-old apprentice in 1932, he was the nation's leading jockey. A year later, Westrope became the first to win 300 races in a single season. By 1940, the 92-pound man described by United Press International as "little pug-nosed, freckle-faced Jack Westrope from the plains of Montana" was a national champion. His popularity was enhanced by his 1939 marriage to actress Nan Grey and living next door to Oliver Hardy of Laurel & Hardy fame in California. In all, Westrope rode 2,467 winners in the U.S. and Cuba, including a final two races before he died in his prime in 1958 after being thrown from a horse named Well Away against a rail at Hollywood Park. Westrope, whose older brother William was killed in a race at Agua Caliente in 1928, died of internal bleeding. He was 40. Westrope was enshrined in the National Museum of Racing and Hall of Fame in Saratoga Springs, New York, in 2002.

Willow Creek

BOB MCLEAN

BASKETBALL

An all-round athlete at a school best known for the small-town basketball novel *Blind Your Ponies*, McLean is Willow Creek's all-time leading scorer, putting up 2,027 points and averaging 21.1 per game from 1967-71. At the state track meet in 1971, he set the state Class C high hurdles record on a Friday morning with a 15.0 mark and then broke it at 14.9 in the afternoon. McLean also was a top-flight long jumper and triple jumper. He eventually became a basketball coach at Twin Bridges.

Wilsall

LARRY MCCLUNG

TRACK AND FIELD

The Wilsall High product did split shifts at Western Montana College, finishing sixth in 1952 in the 800 meters at the NAIA national track and field championships. McClung left Dillon but when he returned 10 years later he established conference records in the 800, mile- and two-mile runs. His 4:23.2 mile in 1964 remains a school record. McClung eventually coached track and cross country in Shelby, leading the Coyotes to state championships in both and twice earning state Coach of the Year honors. He now resides in Livingston, where he sells insurance. McClung was inducted into the Montana Western Hall of Fame in 1983.

Winifred

AMY MECKLING

BASKETBALL

The left-handed point guard led the Raiders to three Class C state titles and a 106-4 record over four years (1993-96), earning MVP honors twice and all-state honors four times. Meckling also was a standout sprinter and solid javelin thrower for the track team. She then starred in basketball at Montana State, where she led the Big Sky Conference in scoring her senior season. Meckling ranks 16th in MSU history in points with 1,233, is second in 3-point shots for a career and shares the school mark for treys in a game (7). Her 238 3-pointers attempted in 2000-01 are a program record and she has the second-best free-throw percentage for a season. She lives in Hamilton.

Winnett

MARTHA DEMBEK

BASKETBALL

A do-everything athlete, Dembek was a three-time all-state selection in basketball from 2010-13. She was all-state in track and cross country six times, winning the long jump and triple jump at the Class C state meet as a freshman and repeating the performance in the long jump as a sophomore. Winnett's valedictorian and academic all-state, Dembek was all-state a combined six times in cross country and track. She went on to play basketball at Montana Tech, where she made an immediate impact. As a senior in 2017, she joined Montana Tech's 1,000-point club and earned honorable mention All-America honors. Dembek finished her career among the Orediggers' top 20 in scoring. She is a certified nurse in Lewistown.

Winston

JESSE AND LINDSAY KRUSE

RODEO

A saddle bronc rider originally from Great Falls, Jesse Kruse was rookie of the year on the PRCA tour in 2007 and a world champion in 2009—the first Great Falls cowboy to accomplish the feat. A Montana graduate, he has qualified for the National Finals Rodeo three times. Kruse, a sprinter on the track team at Great Falls CMR, is a five-time Montana Pro Rodeo Circuit Finals champion. In college at the University of Montana, he was a top all-around cowboy who qualified for the College National Finals Rodeo, finishing second to Ty Murray in saddle bronc riding in 2007. Kruse, who has struggled with injuries in recent years and finished 26th in the world standings in 2019, lives in Winston with his wife, Lindsay, an accomplished barrel racer who has multiple circuit championships in her own right.

Photo: Lindsay Kruse

Wisdom

MIKE PETTIT

RODEO

In the 1980s and '90s, Pettit was a fixture at or near the top the Montana Pro Rodeo Circuit and PRCA leader board in steer wrestling. A 145-pound wrestler in high school at Dillon, Pettit was president of the school's Future Farmers of America chapter. He later was a standout with the Montana State rodeo team as well, winning the all-around crown in a competition against Northwest College in 1978.

Wise River

BOBBY BEERS

FOOTBALL

Though a graduate of Hellgate High in Missoula, where his father, Bob, coached at Montana, Beers' formative years were in Wise River, where he was a dominant grade-school and junior high track athlete in the mid-1980s. A football standout and wrestler at Hellgate, he attended Western Montana College, where he became one of the school's greatest wide receivers. Beers was an All-American and set nine school records, helping lead the Bulldogs to their first NAIA playoff appearances in 1994 and '95. He eventually coached at Columbia Falls and became an assistant at San Jose State and Montana State. Beers then coached for two years with the Berlin Thunder of NFL Europe, after that with the Colorado Crush of the Arena Football League, and is now a scout with the Denver Broncos. He was inducted into the Montana Western Hall of Fame in 2005.

Wolf Creek

FANNIE SPERRY (STEELE)

RODEO

Sperry was born in 1887 on the family homestead at the foot of Beartooth Mountain near Wolf Creek. At the first Calgary Stampede in 1912 she won the first of her two world saddle bronc championships, riding a bronc named Red Wing that had killed a cowboy four days earlier; a year later she duplicated the feat at the Winnipeg Stampede. Famous for riding the "wildest broncos wearing a scandalous divided skirt" and riding them "slick" instead of "hobbled," according to the Montana Historical Society's Ellen Baumler, Sperry later became a rodeo performer with Buffalo Bill Cody and was one of the first three women inducted into the Rodeo Hall of Fame in 1975. Sperry, who also was exceptional with a rifle, was the first Montana native enshrined in the National Cowgirl Hall of Fame. She died in 1983.

Wolf Point

WILLIE WEEKS

BASKETBALL

Weeks didn't leave Wolf Point as its all-time leading scorer—that's Bill Smith, with 1,362 points—but no Wolves athlete is more revered or celebrated. Also known as White Bear, Weeks led Wolf Point to a 43-8 record in his final two seasons, guiding the Wolves to the Big 32 championship in 1968 and earning high school All-America honors along the way. In 1969, Weeks was again an All-American and the only unanimous selection to the Montana Coaches Association Big 32 All-State team. A 6-4 guard, he averaged 18.1 points per game in his career at Montana State, putting him in the top five all-time. At MSU, Weeks was all-Big Sky and an academic All-American. He quit the team briefly as the leading scorer his junior year to attend the College of Great Falls, then returned to finish his career under a new coach. Weeks subsequently earned a tryout with the San Diego Conquistadors and coach Wilt Chamberlain of the old American Basketball Association as well. Weeks, who died in 2006 at age 55, was inducted into the Montana Indian Athletic Hall of Fame in 2008.

Worden

RANDY WALTER

BASEBALL

A three-sport standout at Huntley Project High School, Walter made his name in baseball, starring with the American Legion Billings Royals (1997-99) before three standout seasons as an outfielder at Wichita State. In 1999, he was a Collegiate Baseball High School All-American after hitting .441 with 17 homers and 61 RBIs in 65 games for the Royals. Walter was drafted by the Tampa Bay Devil Rays in the 49th round in 1999. A year later, the Lewistown native was taken in the ninth round by the San Francisco Giants after batting .365 with 10 home runs during his junior year. He retired after six years in the minors. With the Royals, Walter was the state's first and only Legion All-American. In high school, Walter led the Red Devils to Class B state titles in football and basketball, and he was all-state twice in football.

Wyola

CHARLES DILLON

FOOTBALL

A member of the Crow Creek band of the Sioux tribe, Dillon was the focal point of one of the most famous plays in college football history. At the Carlisle (Pa.) Indian School in 1903—the year before the legendary Jim Thorpe arrived—coach Pop Warner cooked up some newfangled plays, including the forward pass, to help his smaller players offset the brute force of opponents. Against powerful Harvard, the Indians unveiled the "hunchback" or "hidden ball" trick. A tailor from a local men's store sewed a pouch in the back of Dillon's uniform and on a kickoff the team formed a wedge and tucked the ball in the pouch. While Harvard scurried about tackling players who pretended to have the ball, Dillon—a lineman who ran the 100-yard dash in 10 flat—went 103 yards untouched; one opponent, thinking Dillon was a blocker, stepped out of the way. Another famous coach, Amos Alonzo Stagg, called the play a "parlor trick" and it was outlawed soon after. Dillon eventually married fellow Carlisle student Rose LaForge of Lodge Grass and became a blacksmith in Wyola.

Zortman

SHANE SCHWENKE

RODEO

One of the state's top team ropers as a header, the Havre native and Harlem High graduate qualified for the National Finals Rodeo four times before retiring in 2011. In 2009, at the Wrangler Canadian Rodeo Tour Championships, Schwenke and teammate Mike Beers set what was believed to be a pro rodeo team-roping record of 3.4 seconds. Schwenke also was the Montana Pro Rodeo Circuit Finals team roping champion as a header in 1990, 1992, 1996, 2003, 2004 and 2010, combining with Kory Mytty of Lolo for 10 titles overall. His retirement was short-lived: Schwenke embarked on a comeback in 2017 at age 50.

Zurich

MIKE TILLEMAN

FOOTBALL

A product of a ranch near Zurich, Tilleman was an all-sports star at Chinook High, where he was a football All-American before moving on to Montana in 1963-64. The 6-foot-7, 270-pounder was a two-time all-Big Sky Conference player and after earning enough credits to graduate eschewed his senior season with the Griz to play in the NFL. Tilleman played with four teams over 12 years, finishing with the Atlanta Falcons in 1976. As a Houston Oiler in 1972, he led the NFL in tackles and quarterback sacks, earning the Brian Piccolo Award as the league's Comeback Player of the Year after overcoming bowel cancer discovered during surgery for a ruptured appendix. A year later, he was all-pro with Atlanta. He returned to the Hi-Line in 1977, buying a car dealership first in Chinook and then in Havre. Tilleman died in September 2020.

Index by Name

Index by Sport

BASEBALL

BASKETBALL

BOXING

FOOTBALL

GOLF

RODEO

SKIING

SLED DOG RACING

TRACK AND FIELD, CROSS COUNTRY

VARIOUS

WRESTLING

About the Author

Jeff Welsch's passion for all things Montana was born during a family station-wagon vacation in 1975, nurtured on frequent trips to the Big Sky State to cover Boise State basketball and Idaho football for The Idaho Statesman in the 1980s, solidified on regular fly-fishing adventures, and ultimately realized with a move to Bozeman in 2004 to become sports editor at the *Daily Chronicle*.

Welsch has been in sports journalism in the western United States for nearly four decades, aside from a six-year hiatus to work for a conservation organization dedicated to protecting the Greater Yellowstone Ecosystem. In 2014, the addictive aroma of newsprint and ink lured him back as sports editor of *The Billings Gazette*, and since August 2016 he has been executive sports editor for the 406mtsports.com website and Lee Montana's four daily newspapers—*The Gazette*, *Missoulian*, *Montana Standard* (Butte) and *Helena Independent Record*.

His numerous state, regional and national reporting awards include first place in the 2006 Associated Press Sports Editors national competition for his burled-arch to burled-arch coverage of one of Montana's Greats: Ennis musher Jessie Royer in Alaska's Iditarod Trail Sled Dog Race.

Welsch has co-authored five books—among them *Backroads & Byways of Montana*, with his wife, Sherry, an endeavor that took them from border to border and heightened their appreciation for their adopted home state. It was the people, places and stories experienced along the way that helped provide the spark for *Montana Greats*.

They have lived in the same home outside of Belgrade for the past 17 years.

"This is the stuff Hollywood movies are made of."
BIG SKY JOURNAL

"I couldn't put it down. It is that good."
BOXINGPROSPECTS.NET

"Elegantly written."
BILLINGS GAZETTE

In the Golden Age of boxing, Montana's Marvin Camel overcame racism, poverty, and isolation to become the first American Indian to win a world boxing title.

Determined to *be someone,* Camel combined extraordinary self-discipline with raw physical power to become the world's first cruiserweight champion. He fought on the same cards as superstars Roberto Duran and Sugar Ray Leonard and never forgot where he came from, proudly wearing his Indian headdress into the ring.

In this gripping biography, author Brian D'Ambrosio captures the drama, danger, beauty, and ugliness of boxing, the hardships of life on an Indian reservation, and the incredible story of a complex and charismatic man who shattered stereotypes, inspired his people, and thrilled boxing fans everywhere with his great warrior heart.

RIVERBENDPUBLISHING.COM